"*The Minding Organization* equips managers to become leaders. It shows that creativity and adaptability are qualities that can be nurtured to create a sense of purpose and enduring competitive value."

—*Paul J. McWhorter,*
Deputy Director, Microsystems, Sandia National Laboratories

"A clear and practical guide to improving and unleashing organizational agility, quick response, the ability to innovate and renew oneself in a constantly changing business world."

—*Juergen W. Ausborn,*
Corporate Vice President & General Manager, Schott Corporation

"Rubinstein and Firstenberg present concepts every manager should know, but so few are even aware of. Fascinating!"

—*Jacques Birol,*
former CEO, Publicis Etoile (France)

"Moshe Rubinstein is one of the world's finest professors and it certainly shows in his newest book, *The Minding Organization* . . . it's a beacon to the modern executive."

—*Bob O. Evans,*
Managing Partner, Technology Strategies and Alliances

"The precepts in *The Minding Organization* direct organizations to be creative and innovative, words that characterize the authors themselves. This is a practical management book by authors with remarkable insights into organizations, into human behavior, and their applications to business."

—*Dr. Victor Tabbush,*
Adjunct Professor, The Anderson School at UCLA

"Rubinstein is one of four true geniuses that I have met in the world. Read this book if you want to improve the results of any creative aspect of your professional life."

—*Todd Lapidus,*
President, Customer, Contact Corporation

"*The Minding Organization* shows how to adapt to constant change by 'bringing the future to the present.' Read it and be inspired!"

—*Theresa Bergjans,*
Systems Engineer, Scitor Corporation

"This book demonstrates how to harness the often dormant intellectual and creative cells in an organization into a mind-set of perpetual energy and power."

—*Michael Rockberger,*
Financial Director, ONDA Publications, Ltd.

"This book is key for any business manager who knows that command and control, hierarchy, and structure are not working, and is looking for a new approach to resolve chaos and ambiguity."

—*Tom Brand,*
Senior Vice President & General Manager, ICI Fiberite (ret.)

The **Minding** Organization

Bring the Future to the Present and Turn Creative Ideas into Business Solutions

---

Moshe F. Rubinstein
Iris R. Firstenberg

John Wiley & Sons, Inc.

NEW YORK • CHICHESTER • WEINHEIM • BRISBANE • SINGAPORE • TORONTO

This book is printed on acid-free paper. ⊚

Published by John Wiley & Sons, Inc.
Published simultaneously in Canada.

This publication is designed to provide accurate and authoritative information in regard to the subject matter covered. It is sold with the understanding that the publisher is not engaged in rendering professional services. If legal, accounting, medical, psychological or any other expert assistance is required, the services of a competent professional person should be sought.

Library of Congress Cataloging-in-Publication Data:

Rubinstein, Moshe F.
    The minding organization : Bring the future to the present and turn creative ideas into business solutions /
Moshe F. Rubinstein, Iris R. Firstenberg.
      p.   cm.
    Includes bibliographical references and index.
    ISBN 0-471-34781-7
    1. Creative ability in business.   2. Organizational change.
3. Uncertainty.   I. Firstenberg, Iris Rubinstein, 1957– .
II. Title.
HD53.R83   1999
658.4'06–dc21   99-22803
                                                  CIP

Printed in the United States of America.

20 19 18 17 16 15 14 13

Dedicated to you, the manager, the leader in the organization, who has demonstrated a spectacular ability to adapt and thrive on the creative edge of chaos.

ACKNOWLEDGMENTS

The ideas and precepts of this book have been presented, discussed, and applied in many organizations all over the world. We have many people to thank for making this possible. Bob Evans, managing partner of Technology Strategies and president of Interactive Voice Systems, provided a fertile ground for testing ideas in the IBM Modern Engineering Programs that he sponsored for a number of years when he served as vice president of IBM; Dave Hanlon, formerly president and CEO of Resorts International; Dan Goldin, administrator of NASA and formerly with TRW; Timothy Hannemann, executive vice president and general manager of the Space and Electronics Group, TRW; Michael Allgeier, president of Hughes' Santa Barbara Research Center; Jose Gasalla, director of executive education, Euroforum, Madrid, Spain; Benedikt Johannesson, president IBM Iceland and president of Talnakonnun,

Iceland; Thornton May, vice president Cambridge Technology Partners; Police Chief Bernard Parks, Los Angeles Police Department; Professor Victor Tabbush, who provided a wide range of opportunities to present and test new ideas on creativity, innovation, and problem solving in scores of programs when he served as director of executive education, Anderson Graduate School of Management, UCLA; Sherri Camps, court administrator, who gave us similar opportunities in programs for judges and court administrators.

Many more people provided opportunities to present and test ideas. They include Professors William Ouchi, John Mamer, Jack McDonough; Carol Scott; Donald Morrison; Robert Andrews, David Lewin, of UCLA; Debra-Lynne Terrill, director of executive education, Anderson Graduate School of Management, UCLA; Professors Schon Beechler and Warren Kirby, Columbia University; Michael Lawler; director of executive programs, University of California, Davis; Jack Garner, bureau chief, Center for Leadership Development, State of California Commission on Peace Officer Standards and Training. Professor Ray Maghroori, Dean College of Business, San Francisco State University, formerly Associate Dean and director executive education University of California, Riverside.

Many organizations in countries all over the world, including Ireland, Italy, France, England, China, Japan, Phillipines, Canada, Israel, Mexico, Yugoslavia, and the United States, gave us the opportunity to interact with people who participated in management and executive education programs. We thank all these organizations and in particular, the program participants, for the feedback they provided and the sparks they ignited that gave birth to ideas incorporated in the book.

Special thanks to our editor at John Wiley and Sons, Renana Meyers, who provided remarkable insights and contributed greatly to both the form and content of the book.

CONTENTS

CHAPTER NINE:
The Minding Organization in Action   173

PROLOGUE

Organizations that have survived the past two decades of turmoil, and are thriving, have demonstrated a spectacular ability to adapt. They embraced total quality management (TQM), continuous measurable improvement (CMI), they downsized, right-sized, reengineered, embarked on cost containment campaigns, introduced integrated product design teams, integrated service teams, embraced diversity in the workplace, advocated change in corporate culture, preached acting locally and thinking globally, adopted global business outlooks, empowered, inspired, motivated, trained, partnered, transformed into learning organizations, introduced new products and new services—and with all that, organizations managed to form mergers, make acquisitions, consolidate some parts of the organization, and spin off others. In short, these thriving organizations have operated on the edge of chaos in their ongoing effort to adapt in the face of new opportunities for change.

Now it appears that even more change is coming, and it is unfolding at a rate more rapid than ever before. To keep up with the complexity and uncertainty of an unconventional and largely unpredictable global business world, organizations must embrace a new metaphor that will transform an organization into a minding organization. The minding organization behaves like a living organism, in which adapting is central to vitality and survival.

Every individual has a mind, used to perceive, judge, make decisions, and adapt. Every minding organization also has a mind, and the manner in which the mind of the organization is developed and deployed determines the success of the organization. The analogy between the human and the minding organization begins with the mind. Just as the human is an organism, so is the minding organization—in fact, the word "organization" comes from the word "organism." An organism has a clear sense of purpose and adapts with agility to changes, both internal and external, to achieve its purpose. For example, an overriding purpose of the human organism is survival. When you plan to cross a busy intersection, you follow certain rules that are part of your survival plan: you look both ways and watch the traffic lights. One day as you begin to cross the street according to plan, your intuition tells you that a car, rapidly approaching from the left, is going to run the red light. You quickly adapt, change your plan, and jump back on the curb. Your ability to rapidly adapt and change your plan midcourse saves your life as, indeed, the car careens through the intersection without stopping.

The minding organization must develop similar strategies. Overly rigid and detailed planning must give way to a strategy that combines less planning and more adapting. A metaphor for this change is the difference between two modes of transportation: railroads and taxi cabs. The railroads were designed with rigid rules, tracks that determined the routes available to customers were laid down, timetables determined when customers could get on and off, and stations that determined where customers could get on and off were built. There was no room for flexibility in the plan. In sharp contrast, taxi-cabs plan far less. Cabs cruise the city, seemingly at random, but in fact they concentrate their efforts in areas where customers are more likely to need them. They have no idea when a customer will call, where the customer will be, or where the customer will want to go. The taxi system is designed to embrace this chaos and uncertainty and to thrive in an environment that is unpredictable.

The minding organization must have a sense of purpose, and articulate the sense of purpose throughout. The minding organization must focus on the future it wants to create. Once the purpose is clearly articulated, the minding organization begins the process of becoming a living organism. This book describes a framework for thinking and provides the tools for a minding organization to emerge. It provides ideas, thinking processes, and patterns of behavior to create an adaptive organization with a requisite variety of unplanned responses to meet an uncertain future laden with surprises—to create a minding organization that learns to bring the future to the present.

The emerging minding organization will:

- Thrive in a business world of chaos and uncertainty, and embrace chaos and uncertainty as a strategy

- Think backward, from the future to the present, and bring the future to the present

- Distribute decision making in such a way that everyone in the organization has the responsibility to be right and the authority to be wrong, as they adapt creatively to an uncertain future

- Use strategies to enhance the creativity and innovation of every member of the organization

- Make errors an organizational strategy, deliberately forcing them to surface where and when they can be used to benefit the organization

- Cultivate mutual trust, respect, honesty, loyalty, and personal integrity

- Create an environment in which the human spirit can soar

The Minding Organization

CHAPTER

1

The Minding
Organization

Organization comes from the word *organism*, which means a
vital, alive being. An organization alive with the ideas and
commitment of its people is an organism. The minding
organization flourishes on dedicated, committed behavior,
which comes from shared perceptions, common goals, commitment to comply with organizational goals, and a relentless striving for improvement. The minding organization balances chaos
and order with a high tolerance for errors as an opportunity to
learn and develop new varieties of responses. Just as the human
organism is able to respond to an array of changes in the environment, the minding organization develops a requisite variety
of responses, planned and unplanned, to cope with uncertainty
as the future unfolds and becomes an unanticipated present.

What exactly is a mind? We know what we mean when we
say that someone is "out of their mind" or has "lost their

mind"—they are behaving in ways that we cannot interpret through any frame of reference, or they are acting contrary to a previously stable frame of reference. We make a similar judgment about organizations. Certain companies appear to have their act together, we can predict their behavior, it makes sense, and we seek out their business. Other companies seem more like the right hand doesn't know what the left hand is doing, we treat them as either having no mind or having lost their mind, and we avoid doing business with them.

In a minding organization, not only does the right hand know what the left hand is doing; it knows without constantly having to supervise the left hand's actions. Just as your body is an organism, and you can reach behind your head with your left hand and catch it with your right, so can a minding organization coordinate its efforts as a single organism.

Staying with the analogy of hands, if you burn one hand on a stove, the mind registers that hot stoves must be avoided, and perpetuates the knowledge by passing it through the organism. The other hand does not hit the burned hand and tell it what an idiot it is for getting burned; rather, it soothes the burned hand and learns from the documented knowledge so that it does not need to also get burned. When people in an organization make mistakes, it is the equivalent of getting burned.

What we do with mistakes as an organization is entirely a function of the mind of the organization. We can choose to punish errors or we can choose to learn from them. If mistakes are punished, then people will quickly figure out ways to hide them, or dismiss them as aberrations from the norm. They will quickly be put out of mind. If, instead, the organizational frame of reference perceives error as an opportunity to improve, mistakes will be studied, patterns may be found, and as a result changes in behavior and thinking may ensue. This information becomes part of the mind of the organization. All minds in the system become aware, just as all body parts become aware of a burned hand, and the organization can make shifts and improvements. In such an organism, a mistake made by 1 or 2 individuals is not going to be made by 50.

The key is to retain errors in the memory of the organization's mind and perpetuate knowledge of error, all as a means of avoiding their repetition, and as a means of relentlessly improving the organization. How can you know what to do right, if you do not know what is wrong? All learning is predicated on error (we do not say "trial and success"), and to ignore mistakes, to put them out of mind, is to become mindless.

In the minding organization mistakes are broadcast, and to really free people from their negative perceptions of errors, mistakes ought to be celebrated. Of course, no one gets up in the morning and thinks of how many ways they can mess up the day. It is amazing, however, how many of our most important innovations were the result of a plan that went astray— the product of mistakes. Were these aberrations kept hidden, we might not have immunizations, Post-it Notes, or aspartame, to name a few.

How is knowledge shared in an organization? We all know of a lot of ways that do not work: Reports are typed and circulated, only to collect dust on office shelves; memos are left in the "to read" pile; e-mail is glanced at and then deleted, but it is not assimilated; messages on bulletin boards make contact with preoccupied minds. What is lacking in all of these communication systems is the human element.

Information in an organization needs to be shared, needs to become part of the collective memory, and can then be the basis of shared perceptions. The issue is how to retain the information, how to perpetuate it so that knowledge becomes a living entity and part of the corporate identity within each worker in the organization. Information is shared in informal networks, around the office watercooler, next to the microwave as coffee is heating, on the way to the parking lot, and any other place where people have a moment to stop and talk. Creating an environment in which people have these opportunities transforms organizations almost overnight. In one organization, a dining hall was created so that people would eat lunch together in small groups and talk. In a university setting, small offices were built around a large, comfortable lounge, encouraging people to come out of their cubicles and be around other people. Thus, the first step in communications is to create the physical environment that allows for it. We have all seen the cartoons of people huddled around the watercooler, hushing so that the boss won't catch them talking. This is the reality in many workplaces. To see how ingrained our prejudices are, imagine walking into an office to find an individual deep in thought with papers spread everywhere about. You would assume that he or she was hard at work. Imagine the same person standing in the hallway talking to two colleagues. Your first impulse is to assume that this person is now not working. We just do not see the connection between conversations and productivity. The truth of the matter is that conversation propels creativity and innovation, and in mindful organizations exchanges among workers is invited, encouraged, and rewarded.

Do we need to change the culture of an organization to make it a minding organization? Changing a culture is not a requirement. Changing a culture is a monumental upheaval that can be years in the making. An organization can become minding well before this transformation. In fact, the process involved in the transformation of a culture requires a process of minding the needs and goals of a company or group. What is needed is a common purpose, which becomes the pulling force, guiding all behavior toward its achievement. What is needed is a subculture centered around a shared sense of purpose.

The Santa Monica Freeway Story

The following is a remarkable example of minding: identifying a purpose, developing a team, acting to achieve the purpose, and then disbanding the team to move on to the next project.

On January 17, 1994, a bridge of the Santa Monica Freeway collapsed in the Los Angeles earthquake, leaving millions of motorists without their daily route to work. Traffic in all of Los Angeles was affected as drivers used alternate roads. The city was in total gridlock. Caltrans (California Transportation

Department) officials initially predicted that it would take any-
where from 12 to 18 months to rebuild the damaged freeways.
With the severity of the problem clear to everyone, Caltrans
promised an intensive, do-what-it-takes campaign to restore
the freeway sooner by awarding the contract to a contractor
who committed to a 6-month schedule for restoring the freeway. The final time lag to complete the repairs? Not 18 months,
not 6 months—but 66 days! How was this accomplished? By
using less advance planning, by looking to the future instead of
to the past, by minding the process. It was accomplished by
using concurrent perceptions in which the future is brought to
the present, and creating a team with a shared purpose: complete the project as quickly as possible. The process that made
this project a success will be treated later in the book. One compelling observation is that people were so intent on the purpose
that they were running, not walking, on the job.

   Some of the details are amazing. Caltrans dispatched employees, armed with cartons of plans and specifications, and flew
them to meet with five contractors concurrently, so that everyone received the same information at the same time. Bids were
evaluated and contracts were awarded the same day. The design
team delivered drawings within six days, a job that the team says
normally takes about nine months.

   The normal review process was turned upside down. Bridge
plans normally arrive at Caltrans where they are evaluated
(weeks and even months of delay), and then they are sent for
peer review (more time elapses). Finally, they are sent to contractors for bidding. This time, the contractor was already in
place, and he got the plans in installments as Caltrans approved
them. The peer review occurred as construction began. The risk
was great for unanticipated changes and uncertainty. To com-
pensate, freeway construction ensued with a Caltrans agency
resident engineer and government inspectors at the job site
throughout the project to eliminate work approval delays.

   Unanticipated obstacles did indeed occur. Workers found
old foundations and an abandoned structure, not indicated on
the plans, that had to be removed. Drillers discovered contam-

inated water. Waterlines leaked, causing heavy equipment to sink in the muddy ground. To make up for lost time, construction proceeded 24 hours a day, seven days a week. Because there was so much noise at night, nearby residents complained and a noise barrier was erected.

Residents accepted that some sacrifices on their part were required; the entire city was suffering from the traffic and their own side streets were now major traffic arteries. Knowing the reason why the work had to continue through the nights, and having a stake in the outcome, gave neighbors the resilience to put up with the temporary intrusion. They shared the purpose: complete the project as quickly as possible.

What lessons can we glean from this remarkable achievement? Saying that "necessity is the mother of invention" fails to cover the amount of teamwork, effort, and minding that constituted the rebuilding of the bridge. Had the freeway restoration been completed in six months, people would have congratulated the management that made it possible. Completing the freeway in 66 days went above and beyond invention. People varied in the motivations that drove them to complete the project quickly: monetary bonuses, restoration of neighborhood peace to those residences whose streets were being used as alternative routes, the challenge of beating a timetable. Thus, people do not have to all be in a project for the same reason. Shared visions do not have to coincide with shared motivations. The key attribute that made this remarkable achievement possible was an alignment of designers, contractors, inspectors, officials of the city, state and federal government, and the general public. All were united by a strong commitment to comply with whatever it took to achieve the shared common purpose: complete the restoration as quickly as possible without compromising safety and quality.

The Minding Process

The incremental nature of actions, when carried out mindlessly, can leave us baffled when consequences begin to emerge. Even if we mind the particulars, our lack of forward-sighted mindfulness may come to haunt us. What seems to happen when we take small steps is that once we have chosen the journey's path, we ignore the fact the we may be on the wrong track. At some point, when we are jolted into looking back, we can see how far we may have come and regret the choices we made with now apparent mindlessness.

To be minding, then, is to recognize change as it is occurring. New labels and categories may be required to meet the new realities that are unfolding. It is the nature of the human mind that our thinking requires labels. If we have a label for something, we are able to mentally manipulate the reality; without a label, the class of objects does not even exist for us. Learning a field means, first and foremost, acquiring the jargon that carves out the nature of what is being studied. Minding means carefully evaluating labels to ensure that they are not misguiding our thought processes. The same event can be labeled a number of ways, each label sending our thoughts in different directions. Imagine a new employee, who is labeled by personnel as determined and hard working. Those same qualities can be described as stubborn and rigid. Our attitude toward the employee will be a function of the labels we use to interpret and categorize his behavior.

The fact that perception of reality is a function of interpretation means that different points of view are going to be part of every interaction. Unless we are consciously minding the process, we tend to lose awareness that there are views other than our own, and that there may be multiple ways of viewing a situation. It is possible that some or all of these views have validity. A team may be working on an assignment that one member views as a challenge, one member views as a burden, and a third views as a piece of cake. Each perspective is valid as an interpretation of the reality through the frame of mind brought to the situation by the individual team member. It is not a question of right versus wrong; rather, it is an issue of achieving goals by minding the realities as interpreted and created by the people involved.

A wonderful anecdote that illustrates this facet of frames of mind and thinking involves an encounter that Moshe had in Jerusalem with an educated, well-to-do Arab named Ahmed. Ahmed put forth the following question to test the wisdom of those gathered at his dinner table: "Imagine that you, your mother, your wife, and your child are in a boat, and it capsizes. You can save yourself and only one of the remaining three. Whom will you save?" The response most common along Western lines of thought is to save the child. The rationale people give is that the child has an entire life ahead and thus has the most to lose. Ahmed, however, considered this to be the wrong answer. As he saw it, there was only one correct answer, with a corresponding rational argument to support it. "You see," he said, "you can have more than one wife in a life-time, you can have more than one child, but you only have one mother. You must save your mother."

Understanding that other people have valid interpretations and points of view that are different from your own is important for a number of reasons. It removes the necessity of trying to convert everyone to the same point of view. Instead, every member of the group accepts the possibility of the various per-spectives and remains open to new information, which may lend more credibility to one or another of the views. When a single-minded perspective is adopted, new information tends to be discounted, or ignored altogether, when it does not fit this frame of mind. Even as evidence mounts, if it does not fit the cognitive model that a person holds, the information will dissi-pate into mindlessness. When we are open to multiple points of view, information is evaluated in a more minding frame, to see where it might fit in. As change occurs, it is brought in incre-mentally and we are not shocked into uttering, "How could I have been so blind!" having looked without seeing.

In the realm of organization and teamwork, when every member of a group shares the same mind-set, mindlessness also easily sets in. For the entire group to be of one frame of mind can be as debilitating as for a single person to maintain only one perspective. The individuals in the group close themselves off to new information and feedback. When we accept the idea that multiple viewpoints may be valid to interpret a situation, we gain multiple ways in which to respond. We spend less time defending our positions, and more energy creating varieties of responses.

What happens when two perspectives are polarized and mutually exclusive? With a truly minding framework, even two opposing interpretations can peacefully coexist in a single mind. You prepare for both options and seek out more information. You stay on your toes, ready to leap in the opposite direction if need be. Once you have chosen a particular path, there is absolutely no requirement to stick to that track if incoming information says to turn around. You will have a less traumatic time making the change if you have been considering this as an option from the outset. Paradoxes and contradictions lead to creative tension, which sparks ideas for new frames of reference, permitting opposites to coexist. An object cannot be stationary and moving at the same time; however, if we consider two frames of reference, the contradiction disappears. A person standing on a moving escalator is moving when viewed from the floor, and is stationary when viewed by a person next to him on the escalator.

Minding means being aware that there is a process that precedes a result. When we look at a successful benchmark of an industry, we don't see the efforts, false starts, errors, setbacks, and other characteristics of every human endeavor. Once we consider the process that produced the results, it does not mean we should follow exactly the same process—it means that we, too, need to create a process that we can live with, a process that will be open to new information, multiple interpretations, and tolerant of error and false starts.

Once a process is chosen, the typical attitude is that the hard part is over. A lot of thought goes into a decision, and then the mind is set on mental autopilot; carrying out the decision is the easy part. Unfortunately, this is a job half done. Once a process is chosen, minding must increase, both to mind the process itself, and any outside information or internal feedback that can alert the need for modifications in the process. For example, consumers spend a certain amount of effort to determine which insurance agency to work with to insure their homes and cars. However, once the choice is made, how often is it evaluated? Premiums are paid mindlessly, unless some major event motivates a renewed evaluation of the original choice. Sure, we may complain that we think our premiums are exorbitant, but how often do we check to see what our other options are? Businesses choose to work with a bank or supplier, and the same mindless loyalty may cost unnecessary money and efforts. Although our original choices may have been made in a mindful way, the continuing process must also be carried out in a minding manner.

When we do not question the process, minding has stopped. Ellen J. Langer, in her insightful book *Mindfulness*, relays the anecdote of three generations of women who have been making pot roast with the same recipe. The youngest woman has always cut a piece off the roast before putting it into the pot. When asked by a friend why she does this, she realizes that she has no idea why it is necessary to cut off a slice, and calls her mother to inquire. Her mother is also puzzled by the question, and she tells her daughter that she cuts off a slice because that's the way her mother has always done it. They decide to question the grandmother on this ritual. The grandmother answers that the reason she slices the roast is, "that's the only way it will fit into my pot." This anecdote illustrates the absurdity of certain actions, which may have a reason for their origin, but are then propagated mindlessly. Many organizations will frequently turn down a new process because "we've never done that before," and will continue with a line of action "because that's the way we've always done it." It may very well be that the organization developed a behavior of "a pot that was too small," but the original reason for the action has become obsolete or irrelevant. "Because we've always done it that way" is synonymous with not minding the content in which you do business. Always ask, "Why?"

A lack of minding is the application of whatever new business theory is in vogue, simply because it is there. Adopting a line of action just because everyone else in the industry is doing it is no different from cutting the slice of roast because Mom did it. Minding your own business literally means evaluating any process, whether it is one that you have been using for a long time, or one that everyone is currently praising and gung-ho about, and assessing whether there is a reason for you to use it.

Is there a point at which minding becomes incapacitating? After all, we certainly cannot call every insurance company every day to see what rates they might offer us; we cannot question every aspect of every business move; at some point, we have to accept our decisions and move on. Minding does not mean that we never accept a decision and move on. It means, instead, that we are conscious that we have done so and that the decision was, in this sense, arbitrary; that is, we choose a cutoff point where we stop asking questions and seeking additional information. This mind frame will allow change to more readily be admitted; it does not mean that we will constantly be changing. By minding, we continue to be aware of choices, aware that other alternatives are available, even if at the moment we are not availing ourselves of them. Minding is then a liberating activity, not an incapacitating activity. When changes do become necessary, they are not viewed as departures from the norm, but as part of the greater norm.

Our decisions are not based on all possible data because this is physically impossible. Incorporating the notion that there are multiple valid perspectives, we understand that there are multiple possible right answers. For some, the least cost is the right answer; for others, the shortest response time; others may have yet other criteria. A decision that is right in one context may not be appropriate in another. By minding the process of making a decision, we can allow ourselves the luxury of changing our minds without trauma. The decision itself takes on less aura than the process that gets us to it.

The emphasis on process rather than exclusively on results is not easy for a society that values achievements. Promotions and raises are based on the bottom line, not on lines of thought. A story to illustrate this point: A farmer who is the father of two sons finds himself too ill to till his fields. He calls the first son to his bedside and asks him to work the fields. The son caresses his father and assures him that he will tend to the work. However, as soon as he leaves his father he takes the family car and spends the day in town, thinking his father will never know the difference. The father calls the second son and asks him to also tend the fields. The second son irately responds that he is tired of farm work and refuses to take on the burden. When he leaves his father's bedside, he reflects for awhile and is ashamed of himself. Without saying a word to his father, he goes out to the field and does the entire job. At the end of the day, the father discovers the first son spent the day carousing in town while the second son tilled the field. Which son incurs more of the father's anger on this day? It is, of course, a matter of perspective. In Western society most people would answer that the first son, who promised to work but failed to do so, would get the bulk of the father's anger. The second son, while speaking disrespectfully to his father, nevertheless got the job done. The emphasis is on the outcome. In another culture, in which process takes precedence over results, the emphasis is on how the sons spoke to their father. People from a process-oriented culture will be more angry with the son who spoke spitefully, with the ensuing fieldwork of secondary importance. Once again, there is always more than one way to look at a situation.

Errors as Part of the Minding Process

Using a process orientation rather than an outcome orientation, the frame in which we view errors will change. An error is not an outcome; rather, it is part of the process. It is not an endpoint on which we dwell, but a junction that must be articulated and connected to the journey. Processes are subject to continuous revision; outcomes are rigid. This is the most significant difference in the two approaches. Error as part of an ongoing process implies that we learn, adapt, and move on; error as an outcome freezes us in place.

The dynamic nature of process by definition implies unpredictability and unreliability. When something occurs that we did not expect in advance, we call it an error. Whereas the gap between expectation and what occurs can be either negative or positive, we dwell on the negative and spend time, money, and other resources to increase reliability of systems, all to reduce the possibility of error. Yet, unreliability remains a problem, no matter what we do to contain it. The most significant source of unreliability in even the most sophisticated systems is the human element. Machines are designed by humans, inspectors of systems are themselves human, as are the inspectors of the inspectors. Stupidity is rarely the source of the problem. Ironically, the one thing we can depend on in any system is that human error will surface. We should recall more often the words of Alexander Pope: "To err is human." Anything touted as foolproof, or perfect, fails a primary test of minding: the human.

People who design products and services must be vigilantly open to new perspectives and changes in context. Evolutionary changes are slow and rooted in habitual thinking; revolutionary innovations are fast and rooted in spontaneous thinking. Where, however, do the ideas for revolutionary changes come from? One of the best places to get such ideas is from a study of human error.

The world is full of good design, but we are unaware of most of it. Poor design catches our attention because a product is awkward to use or a service frustrating to implement. Details that make a product work are added by people carefully thinking of how others use objects, the kinds of errors that can ensue, and carefully observing the interaction between people and products. When someone makes an error, there is usually a good reason for it. Perhaps the information available is incomplete or misleading. Perhaps the context leads to a misinterpretation of available information. Most decisions seem sensible at the time they are made. Errors are understandable once their cause is determined. Systems must be designed to learn from error, not just eliminate it.

Systems need not be complex for designers to carefully monitor and consider error. How many times have you pulled on a door that was supposed to be pushed, and it even had the word "push" written in bold letters across the handle? The problem lies not with the user, but with the design of the door. The design of the door and handle should give a user enough information to know what to do, without resorting to written instructions. How often do you use a copy machine and walk off, leaving the original inside the machine? We berate ourselves for being absentminded, when in reality, the design of the machine almost asks for it. Donald Norman, in a delightful book called *The Design of Everyday Things*, takes issue with a multitude of objects whose designs fail to consider the human factor. Norman encourages designers to plan for error, to think of each action by a user as an attempt to step in the right direction. Human cognition is limited, and ability to interact with objects is subject to constraints. A designer who depends on an instruction manual to mediate between a product and a user has not been creative enough to consider alternatives.

The Importance of Context and Reframing

A critical component of minding is the context in which a situation is embedded. In our organizations, circumstances dictate the value of information, its relevance, and its truth. For example, consider the idea that a lawyer must be party to every business contract. Is this always true? Western companies that tried to set up contracts with Japanese businesses and brought their lawyers to the negotiations quickly found that the new context, namely business with another culture, dictated new truths. In the Japanese mind-set, bringing in a lawyer symbolizes lack of trust, which is insulting and unacceptable.

Likewise, information that is relevant in one context may be irrelevant in another context. Many medical diagnoses depend on tests which may be costly and painful, but which are undertaken to understand the cause of problematic symptoms. These tests are relevant when a course of treatment depends on the outcome of the tests. In 1974, our 85-year-old grandfather fell into a coma, and doctors ordered tests to determine the cause. The question these doctors should have asked themselves is whether knowing the cause was relevant to the current case. When questioned by the family, the doctors admitted that knowing the cause of the coma would not change the treatment and that, in fact, the test itself had the potential to cause additional bodily damage. The tests were not undertaken, because although they would provide medical information, it would be irrelevant information. We are happy to say that our grandfather made a miraculous recovery from his coma and lived to the age of 98 in amazing health.

The context will determine how we interpret what may otherwise be the same information. If we see two men punching and hitting each other, our reaction will depend on whether it is happening in the lobby of our business, or as part of a boxing match. Our own behavior is determined by context; we behave differently at a table when eating at a fast-food restaurant compared with an elegant, expensive restaurant. If we are at an elegant restaurant with business clients, we may behave differently than if we are at the same restaurant with an old college buddy.

Context is a powerful controlling mechanism, and minding requires an awareness of its effects. What role do our perceptions play in creating context? Context, like any other aspect of reality, is also a function of our interpretations. Are the economics of today a good context for starting a business? This depends on what factors you are considering and what type of business you are evaluating. Is childbirth painful? When a woman interprets the sensations of childbirth in the context of a natural process that her body is creating, contractions will be interpreted and acted upon in a different way than when those same sensations are seen in the context of an uncontrollable, unnatural force. When we perceive that someone has taken our words "out of context," we are really saying that they have imposed a context on our words that is different from the context we framed for our words.

The ability to change contexts and use multiple contexts is also known as reframing. At the concrete level, we carefully choose the frames for photos we cherish to do justice to the picture. We know that a cheap, gold-plated frame from the drugstore will create a different effect than an elegant, thick, sterling silver frame from Tiffany's. Likewise, the frame in which we couch ideas will have an effect on our interpretation of the information. As we increase our repertoire of mental frames, we increase our agility to interpret information and innovate. Railroads declined because they saw themselves in the limited context of "moving on rails," and not in the broader frame of "transportation." Typewriter companies became obsolete because they restricted themselves to "typing" instead of the broader frame of "word processing." In contrast, Xerox reframed itself to become "The Document Company" by broadening the context from the limits of being "The Photocopy Company." Telephone companies today are reframing the way they see themselves, from the frame of "oral communication" to the frame of "global synapses," connecting across people much like the connections of the nervous system within the human. Interpreting a business through new frames opens up possible ventures that the mind otherwise never considers. Narrow frames give way to wider frames; vertical frames give way to horizontal frames; single-dimension frames give way to frames of two and three dimensions. The possibilities are endless for increasing minding.

A New Metaphor

This book provides a new metaphor for organizations to make it possible to emulate the Santa Monica Freeway story as a way of life in the organization. The old metaphor for the organization was the railroad, with its fixed plans, fixed rails and stations, and fixed time schedules. The new metaphor is that of taxi cabs, cruising surface streets with only partial plans, to meet needs as the future unfolds, making decisions as closely as possible to the time when action must be taken, and made by a driver on the spot, consistent with the passenger's needs. In the old metaphor, the organization made plans in advance and the passengers had to adjust their plans accordingly. In the new metaphor, the organization must adjust in real time to the passengers whose plans are unknown most of the time.

The new metaphor requires the organization to embrace uncertainty and chaos, and to learn to thrive on it. The organization must find ways to bring the future closer to the present by employing concurrent perceptions, those of the past, present, and future, and learn the powerful skills of thinking backwards. Decision making must become more distributed across the organization, all the way to the "vehicle driver." Learning will be central if the organization continues to adapt and becomes capable of dealing with the unplanned and unanticipated, which will be more prevalent in the future.

The central role of leadership in the new organization will shift from technical problem solving to adaptive, creative problem solving. The organization will require leadership that can operate on the edge of chaos by relinquishing command and control and creating an environment of mutual trust and respect. The new leadership must develop people with an adaptive capacity to work creatively in a changing world and provide them with a sense of purpose. Purpose pulls all the trajectories of motion in the complex organization into a shared orbit.

The Age of the Brain

The new millennium is introducing a new age to management science. Whereas in the past people had lots of time but little information and limited access to information, today we are chronically short of time and have access to a wealth of information. A seventeenth-century English gentleman was likely exposed to less information in his entire lifetime than there is today in a single edition of a daily newspaper. In the new age change is rapid, with chaos and uncertainty an integral part of our lives. We must learn to live harmoniously with change, chaos, and uncertainty. It is now the age of the brain. It is the age of finding ways to tap more of the human potential for creativity and innovation, to learn to adapt to chaos and uncertainty, and to use our minds to establish a sense of purpose and meaning in our personal and professional lives. The future is unfolding and quickly becoming an unanticipated present.

The Power of Human Perception

The human brain has been described in many ways in the history of science. Early description used the engine as the model of the brain, then came the telephone switchboard model. During the period of World War II, the servomechanism model of dynamic feedback and control was used to describe the functions of the brain. When the digital computer made its appearance, it offered a new model for the brain as an information-processing machine that can create, store, and retrieve information. The emphasis in all these models was focused on flow of information and sequential operations performed by the brain through the use of rules of logic. The computer as a model of the brain became so powerful that it led to the new field of artificial intelligence (AI), which endeavors to mimic human intelligence. The programs of AI moved from early efforts, with simple games such as tic-tac-toe, to sophisticated chess-playing programs and programs to understand newspaper editorials in specialized fields.

Artificial intelligence has made a profound contribution to enhance our understanding of the power and complexity of the human brain. It has also identified the limits of the computer as the model of the brain. Once we move out from the expert domain to the domain of common sense, it is virtually impossible to mimic human behavior. Unpredictable events that require improvisation are still a domain in which the human reigns supreme, and the computer can hardly begin to emulate successfully.

Expert systems, which are computer programs that attempt to mimic expert behavior, are based on the assumption that the expert has a complete theory that he or she can articulate. However, evidence is mounting that experts operate with incomplete theories, and they must balance constancy of behavior with flexibility to adapt to new situations by improvising. Also, the expert is not able to articulate fully the process that he or she employs. More recently, workers in the field of neural networks have claimed that such a network, when it models the biological structure of the brain, will be able to mimic the expert more closely by learning to improvise and learning to do that which the expert cannot describe in the form of rules.

Artificial intelligence and expert systems continue to serve as powerful models for some aspects of human intelligence in many areas, and many functions that we ascribe to human logic will be taken over more and more by the digital computer or possibly by neural networks. This suggests that, in the age of computers, humans should place more emphasis on perception, namely the ability to gain knowledge through our senses of sight, hearing, smell, taste, and touch. The logical skills of the brain have evolved for 2 million years, whereas the sensory and motor skills have evolved over several hundred million years. The logical skills can be performed much more efficiently by the computer once the rules are known, but the skills of perception are difficult for the computer to mimic. Just think of how quickly you recognize a friend and how difficult it would be to articulate how you did it, let alone write a computer program to do it in a way that would match your skills. We all recognize people even after years of not seeing them, and manage to do so despite major changes in features, such as complete hair loss or a "new" nose. This ability to acquire and interpret information through our senses is most amazing.

The new age requires that we make more effective use of our powers of perception in learning, problem solving, and in enriching the acquisition and potential meaning of information channeled through our senses. The machines of the industrial revolution amplified human muscles, and caused a shift from focus on manual work to work with the brain. The computer of our information age is amplifying intelligence by performing logical operations and freeing us to focus more attention on the use of human perception.

The focus in learning, planning, and problem solving should be on heightened perception. More breadth and more depth in the ways we can look and see have the potential of improving the quality and quantity of our ideas, thoughts, and actions.

Minding and Creativity

Characteristics of minding come from the same pool of traits as the characteristics of creativity. People who are open to new information, understand multiple perspectives, use a variety of interpretations, and incorporate context as a positive attribute, are both creative and minding.

Creative thinking requires a process that is quite different from that of rational thinking. Whereas rational thinking depends on categories and labels that have been set up in advance, creative thinking demands that we form new categories and labels. Rational thought leads us to find the similarities between a new experience and previous experiences so that we can treat them the same way. Creative thought looks for the differences among experiences, seeking unique ways of both interpreting situations and acting upon them. Rational thinking seeks to confirm; creative thinking seeks to invent. Both rational thought and creative thought are necessary for minding.

Car wash owners have always been plagued by the threat of bad weather. As soon as rain is imminent, people stop coming to wash their cars, and when it actually rains, car wash owners do not even bother opening up for business. The rational way of looking at this confirms their actions. However, a car wash owner in Los Angeles devised a clever advertisement to change the mind-set of car owners to encourage them to wash their cars not only in bad weather, but especially in bad weather! He advertised the negative effect of acid rain on car paint, and how important it is to get the acid rain professionally removed as soon as possible. In effect, he invented a new category as applied to car wash requirements. Advertising as an entire industry seeks to create categories of needs by interpreting situations for consumers in novel ways. The numbers of products that we cannot live without could fill a book, all of which were not advertised because of a perceived need on the part of consumers, but as a need created and invented for consumers by creative advertising.

Creativity

Creativity can find expression in a variety of ways. The discovery of new knowledge, new trends, or new products or services is one expression of creativity. The interpretation of new knowledge and new trends, or the integration of separate pieces of knowledge and different trends into a cohesive whole, are other manifestations of creativity. Identifying business applications or finding new ways of disseminating information are still other types of creativity. There are many more manifestations of human creativity that span the spectrum of the human experience from the technical, economical, ecological, social, emotional, to the spiritual. Harvard psychologist Howard Gardner has developed a theory of multiple intelligences that people have within themselves. They include the following abilities:

- Logical mathematical
- Verbal
- Spatial
- Musical
- Bodily—kinesthetic
- Interpersonal—with others
- Intrapersonal—with oneself

These many forms of intelligence translate to the following possible forms of creativity and excellence in various domains: teaching, research, poetry, mathematics, music, technical, verbal expression, acting, body movement, social behavior, psychology, as well as others.

Attributes of Creative People

The following attributes summarize many studies over the years characterizing people who display creative behavior. Creative people:

- Have a strong capacity for abstract thinking
- Can assimilate opposites
- Have high tolerance for complexity
- Respect facts and attempt to give them interpretation and meaning in a larger context
- Tolerate uncertainty, ambiguity, and conflict
- Like adventure
- Enjoy the surprise of the unplanned
- Are confident in themselves and in what they are doing, whatever the outcome
- Like to see the results of their efforts

Finally, for creative people, optimism and errors are actual strategies.

These attributes are central to the creative process that involves homospatial thinking, which calls for holding opposites in the same space or frame long enough to permit the possible emergence of new frames, new ideas, or new creative sparks. This juxtaposition of opposites, such as negative and positive, right and wrong, good and bad, rest and motion, wave and particle, and so on, is part of the creative process that includes the following oscillations between extremes of spectrums: the state of chaos and the state of order, diffused broad panoramas and sharply focused fields, the whole and its constituent elements, the abstract and the concrete, to see the familiar as strange and the strange as familiar.

Personal Predispositions and the Organization

To function effectively in a complex environment, the organization requires characteristics of behavior that one person cannot exhibit at the same time, yet they may be required in different parts of the organization at the same time. We need more intuition and emotional involvement in the early stages of a new endeavor and more analysis and planning at the final stages. Ned Herrmann, formerly an executive at General Electric, has developed a scale to measure people on four dimensions. The attributes are analysis, intuition, order, and people. A person can be rated low (L), medium (M), or high (H) on each dimension. An engineer would likely rate very high on analysis, an artist on intuition, a bookkeeper on order, and a social worker on people. People can have all four attributes to a larger or lesser degree; however, it is virtually impossible for one person to embrace at the same time high levels of the bookkeeper's discipline of order and the artist's freedom of intuition. Yet both can be present at high levels within the organization—in different people. Isaac Adizes classified management styles in a similar way using four attributes: P—producer of results (compatible with analysis); E—entrepreneur (compatible with intuition); A—administrator (compatible with order); and I—integrator of people (compatible with people).

Integrity of Personality and the Organization

Both thinking skills and people skills are very important to the success of the organization. We need people with diverse abilities and orientations, who interact and thus enrich and strengthen the ability of the organization to learn, grow, thrive, and adapt in a complex, changing environment. Paul McWhorter, from Sandia National Laboratories, suggested in the UCLA program "Creativity and Innovation in the Organization" that the vitality of the organization is very much dependent on four values: trustworthiness, honesty, loyalty, and integrity. The minding organization will have all these values at a high level, manifested in the behaviors of the people who compose the organization. The meaning of these four values as articulated by McWhorter are as follows:

Trustworthiness: Can you depend on me to do what I say? Is my behavior following my talk? Do I follow through on my commitments?

Honesty: Do I tell the truth? Do I seek to embrace the spirit of truthfulness in my reports and communication?

Integrity: Do I do the right thing, even when no one is watching? Do I do the right thing even if it affects (in the short term) my pursuit of critical goals? Do I put doing the right thing above all other goals?

Loyalty: Am I loyal to my company, my boss, my coworkers, and my employees? Do I put the good of others on par with my own self-interest? Do I seek to build others up instead of tearing them down?

The minding organization will live by these values and will embrace the minding process. Only then can the transformation of the organization into an organism begin.

CHAPTER 7

Transforming the Organization into an Organism

Transforming the Organization into an Organism

Complexity as the Basis for Minding

Science is often viewed as a source of complexity. In fact, science is dedicated to the pursuit of simplicity. Science provides models for encapsulating seemingly unrelated observations and giving them meaning in a larger context. For example, Kepler's (1571–1630) model for the solar system is based on three laws. These laws made it simpler to predict the positions of the planets as they revolve around the sun, and when eclipses of the moon and sun will occur.

Isaac Newton (1642–1727) introduced the concept of the gravitational field that both contained and explained Kepler's laws. This model encapsulated more diverse phenomena and observations, such as the motion of the planets, the free fall of objects, oscillation of a pendulum, and the tides in the ocean.

Newton set the stage for modern astronomy with the abstract notion of a gravitational field.

Consider the gravitational field as an attractor. When a space vehicle launched from earth enters a particular orbit around a planet, it will remain there under certain conditions, no matter what trajectory it followed to get into that orbit. If the distance from the planet and the velocity of the space vehicle are just right, it will become a satellite of the planet. Only a supply of energy to change the velocity or position of the vehicle can free it from the attracting orbit.

Newton's model created a revolution in thinking and guided scientific research for more than 200 years. This model has become a metaphor in disciplines and areas of human interest far removed from mechanics and gravity. Newton himself believed that through the study of the gravitational field he would find certainty about the existence of the "cause of all causes," the center of gravity of the universe, where God resides.

The philosopher Immanuel Kant (1724–1804) was very impressed by Newton's concept of the gravitational field and the forces of attraction, which explains the regularity in the motions of the planets, the sun, the moon, and the stars. Kant used Newton's model describing how masses interact in a gravitational field as a metaphor for finding comparable laws of conduct in human affairs. Kant's categorical imperative stipulated a criterion for human behavior that can be likened to the orbital attractors in the gravitational field that guide the planets as they move in their orbits: "Act in such a way, that if others did the same, you would benefit."

This is a group, rather than an individual, rationality. Adherence to such collective rationality implies a strong commitment to mutual trust. If this were possible, mutual trust would become an attractor in human affairs much like the attractors of the field of gravity. Behavioral patterns, or trajectories, would be guided by mutual trust.

The order that is apparent in the Newtonian model became the model for organizations. The orderly machinelike model of the organization persisted for a long time. As new developments in science emerged, they too became metaphors for organization. The Uncertainty Principle suggested limits to what we can observe and predict. Newton's model was augmented by Einstein's theory of relativity. In 1858, Darwin proposed his theory of the origin and perpetuation of species through natural selection and survival of the fittest.

Research in biology and in mathematical theory of complexity is beginning to raise questions about Darwin's model of evolution, just as Einstein's relativity theory did with Newton's model. At the same time, the world we live in is becoming more complex. Organizations are beginning to question the models they have embraced in the past, because they are not working in the present.

The time is ripe for a new metaphor for organizations. The metaphor we shall discuss is the metaphor of the minding organization—how complexity theory can be used to transform an organization into an organism. In such an organism, individual behavior is driven or attracted by a shared purpose. Each individual acts in such a way that if others were to do the same, it would be to the benefit of both the individual and others at one and the same time. People are aligned and bound by mutual trust and driven by common purpose, like the organs within a living, thriving human being.

A biological model coupled with the theory of complexity will help us create a framework for the new organization of the future, as it is beginning to emerge today. Some aspects of this new organization are already in action. The metaphor of an organism for the organization is suitable to describe a growing, changing, renewing organization in which each individual becomes a microcosm of the whole, reflecting the whole through its behavior. Each individual mind mirrors the mind of the organization.

Evolution and Revolution

Charles Darwin published his theory of evolution in 1858. The theory proposed the ideas of natural selection and survival of the fittest. This implied that living forms, including humans, were acts of random variations of natural selection, more like evolving historical accidents than the results of the spontaneous acts of six days of creation as described in the Bible. Since Darwin, natural selection has become known as the process that leads to a transition from chaos to order through slow, random steps of mutation, selection, and survival of the fittest. The theory suggested a contradiction of the biblical stories from the book of Genesis that describe the emergence of spontaneous order that ensued when "God said . . . and God created."

The new science of complexity suggests that order, as described by the model of evolution, is not entirely random and accidental. Natural selection, it suggests, is a refinement process that follows a spontaneous transition from chaos to order. We are familiar with phenomena of spontaneous transition from chaos to order in physical systems. Water molecules moving in chaotic disarray transition spontaneously to ice. Oil dropped on water forms spheres spontaneously. Snowflakes spontaneously assume a symmetrical shape along six axes. However, the idea of a spontaneous transition from chaos to order in complex living systems is new. It suggests the existence of natural laws to explain spontaneous transition from chaos to order to augment natural selection and evolution as a model for the origin of the species and the ensuing order.

The new science of complexity suggests a model of complex systems that go through a rapid transition from chaos to order by self-organizing. Evolution, then, is the process of slowly paced refinements, working within a state of order initially achieved through an act of spontaneous self-organization.

The spontaneous emerging order can be likened to a revolution, or a major breakthrough innovation, whereas evolution involves the refinements of the new level of order resulting from the revolution. In human artifacts, evolution involves design improvements on the basic major breakthrough innovation. Consider bicycles, automobiles, airplanes, and computers. In museums showing the history of technology, we can see hundreds of adaptations and refinements of these artifacts, with the fittest surviving into the next generation of the product. The hundreds of adaptations are not new orders. In all their evolving forms, they remain bicycles, automobiles, airplanes, and computers. They are not a new species, but rather a refinement, however profound and creative the introduced changes are.

The two stages of revolution and evolution are shown schematically in Figure 2.1. The horizontal axis is the timescale. The vertical axis is the scale for the level of order; the higher on the scale, the more order. To transition from one level of order to a new level, a surge of energy is needed to create a spontaneous event of very high impact, a revolution, that can create the lift to a higher state of order.

Self-Organization

Self-organization is most amazing when we think of the process that leads from a fertilized egg to a fully formed human being.

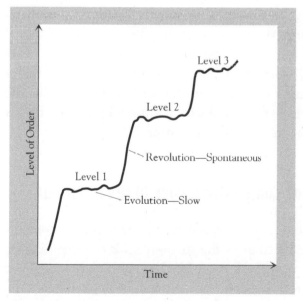

FIGURE 2.1 The two stages of revolution and evolution.

Fifty sequential cell divisions become the staggering number of 1 million billion cells in the newborn. These cells self-organize into 256 known cell types, such as nerve cells, blood cells, kidney, liver, muscle, lung, skin, and so on. The DNA in the nucleus of each cell contains the genetic code. The genetic system contains 100,000 different genes. Different cell types have different genes active in them. For example, the muscle cells have muscle fiber ingredient active in them, whereas red blood cells have hemoglobin. The new science of complexity suggests that the network of cells that leads to the adult human is an order achieved through steps of spontaneous self-organization that occur in complex systems. The 256 known cell types activated by 100,000 genes are not accidental random numbers. The number of cell types resulting from the genes is part of an order that ensues in self-organizing regulatory networks. In theory, the number of ordered clusters, namely cell types, for a sparsely linked network of 100,000 genes is expected to be 317, which is the square root of 100,000 (Kauffman, 1995).

Just watch a child learning to crawl, walk, and talk, to contemplate the complexity of the system and marvel at the capacity for self-organization as it thrives on the edge of chaos, continuing to move to higher levels of order, driven by an innate and compelling force of purpose: the will to adapt and survive. The child progresses with no school for crawling, walking, or talking. It just happens. Later on in life the will to survive gets recharged with additional purposes, the most profound being the will to meaning.

Applying Complexity Theory to Organizations

Because we are going to employ the theory of complexity and self-organization as the metaphor for the organization of the future, we will use a contrived, simple example to illustrate the meaning of key concepts that will be applied later on.

Suppose we provide a person with a miner's helmet. A small battery with an on/off switch is attached to the helmet and is wired to a lightbulb, also on the helmet. Our focus is on the state of the lightbulb. It can assume two states: on or off. If we have two people with such helmets, then the two can assume four different states: one state with both lights on, one with both off, and two states with one bulb on and one off. For three people we will have eight states. Every time we add a person with a helmet, the number of states is doubled. Thus, for n people, there are 2 to the power of n states. For 10 people, for instance, there are 2 to the power of 10, or 1,024, states. One thousand twenty-four distinctly different states for the 10 lights, from all off to all on. The 1,024 states are referred to as the state space of the 10-lightbulb system. The state space for n lightbulbs is 2 to the power of n. The state space encompasses the complete range of possible behaviors that the system can assume.

The state of each lightbulb can be determined by rules of conduct depending on how the people are linked. At the extreme end of the scale, we have no links and each person is free to switch his light on or off independent of what all the others do. In this case, the system of 10 people will be in a state of chaos, in which the system can transition from one state to another, going possibly through any of the state space states. At the other extreme, we could replace the individual batteries on each helmet with one battery and a single on/off switch connected to all the helmets. The switch is then controlled by a dictator who thinks and decides for everybody. Now, only two states are possible: either all on or all off, for all 10 lightbulbs. We have the state of order. Between these two extremes of chaos and order we can have groups of people agreeing to follow some rules of behavior. This will represent a partial connectivity of the system. For example, suppose the 10 people were divided into three groups, which we label A, B, and C. Group A consists of four people, and groups B and C consist of three people each. Each group agrees to act together in such a way that if one or more lights in the group are on, all others are turned on. In addition, each group has established rules of conduct based on the behavior of the other two groups as follows:

- Group A will assume an on state whenever both B and C are on, and assume an off state otherwise.
- Group B will assume an on state if at least one of the other groups (A or C) is on, and assume an off state otherwise.
- Group C will assume an on state if at least one of the other groups (A or B) is on, and assume an off state otherwise.

Adhering to these rules of conduct, the system will settle into one of the following three states in the state space, irrespective of the initial state, which could have been any one of the 1,024 possible states in the state space.

1. All lights are off.
2. A cycle of two states, called a state cycle, in which the system alternates between only Group B on to only Group C on, back to only B on, then only C on, and so on forever.
3. All lights on.

These three resulting final behaviors are called attractors. Attractors are end states that the system flows into or gravitates toward when it starts in some other state. If a system starts in an attractor state, it remains there. The attractor can consist of a single state in the state space, or a repetitive cycle of states called a state cycle. The sequence of states that the system follows from an initial state through intermediate states until it reaches an attractor is called a trajectory. It is somewhat like a spaceship trajectory, passing through many states before it is captured in a gravitational orbit of a planet, then remaining there as its end state, the attractor.

In our example of the three groups of lights, there are eight states in which the groups of lights can be on or off. Of those eight states, if all lights are off for all groups, the system remains in that attractor.

If only group B is on and the other groups are off, the system will be in the state cycle attractor, alternating between B on and then C on. The system will be in this same state cycle attractor if it starts with group C as the only group with its lights on.

All other states in which at least group A is on or both B and C are on flow into the attractor of all lights on.

Thus, 1,024 possible states very quickly land in one of two fixed states or a state cycle. Order is achieved rapidly.

How a Complex System Becomes an Organism

To appreciate the concepts of chaos and order more fully, let us expand the last example from 10 people with miner's helmets and lightbulbs to 200 people. In the state of order, the 200 lights are all on or all off. In the state of chaos, the system will transit from one state to another with no emerging pattern. The state space of 2 to the power of 200 states is such a staggering number that it defies imagination. If this system could transition through 1 million different states in 1 second, it would still take billions and billions of years to go through the entire state space. If this is true of 200 lights, think of the complexity with 100,000 genes or the 100 billion neurons in the human brain.

Between the extremes of chaos and order, the system can self-organize into clusters that follow rules of behavior internally as well as externally, by influencing and being influenced by neighboring clusters. The size of each cluster and the number of clusters will determine where along the scale from order to chaos the system is positioned. Namely, the degree of order will be determined by the number of attractors, and how rapidly they can be reached from any state in the complex environment. To survive in a variable environment, living systems must strike a balance between the stability of order and the instability of change. A system must be stable, but not frozen in one state, nor unstable to the point of quick departures from one state to another as a result of the slightest change in the environment in which the system must adapt to survive.

Studies of complex systems have indicated that systems adapt best when they operate in a state of order on the edge of chaos, in which a measure of stable constancy is coupled with the flexibility of adaptability—that is, where evolutionary, planned, slow, and orderly changes within the state of order, rooted in habitual thinking, are augmented by revolutionary, rapid, breakthrough innovations rooted in unplanned spontaneous thinking.

We deliberately introduced people in our miners'-helmets-and-lightbulbs example, because our focus is on people and organizations that can be transformed into organisms. The attractors in human systems of organization will provide the centers of pull that will channel behavior along trajectories that seek the desired end states.

Coevolution

Systems, or parts of systems in the forms of clusters, do not operate in isolation. They are linked together with other clusters and systems and they coevolve. We invent, shape, change, and refine artifacts; artifacts, in turn, change us. We coevolve with artifacts that we create; we shape them as they shape us. The revolution is in the invention of the artifacts. Once invented and found useful, the reciprocity starts. The artifacts pull people to adopt them because they help attain human goals. Those who do not adopt them fall behind. Major breakthrough innovations and inventions create revolutions that usher new futures for mankind, futures that demand that we coevolve with the innovation or invention at a new level of order. Such were the agricultural, industrial, and now the computer information revolution. The ingenious discovery that seeds hidden from sight in the ground will, with time and care, grow into plants was the beginning of the agricultural revolution. Plants and humans have coevolved ever since, each changing in response to the other. As we chose edible crops over inedible weeds, natural selection increased the proportion of crops to weeds. Coevolution is a form of mutual dependence. We cannot survive without some crops, nor can some of the human cultivated crops survive without our care.

The machines of the industrial age and humans also coevolved. The computer and humans are presently coevolving. Once the computer was invented and found useful, we set out to change the tool as it changes us. We work to make the tool more user-friendly, as we adapt to how this artifact reshapes human life at work and at home. Most profound is the effect of the computer and telecommunications on the links we can form with sources of information and with other humans. We can form relationships without regard to location or distance between ourselves and others. With on-line real-time translation, even language may become less of a barrier, and with on-line real-time interpretation of meaning, culture may also be less of a barrier between people. We are almost at a point at which we can choose the cluster that we wish to be a part of.

What does this mean? What implications will it have on innovation and creativity? How should organizations coevolve with this new artifact and the new choices it provides every person who learns how to use it? How do we align the individuals with the organization? What defines the organization for the individual? Is shared meaning becoming a short-lived state in the state space of a complex system? Or, is it an attractor, stable enough to last through the next revolution? Are we at risk of becoming one large cluster that will destroy the richness of diversity and stifle creativity?

We are in a state of flux. We are on the edge of chaos. It is time for great innovation and creativity to spark ideas for the next revolution. Only with mutual trust can we remove the blocks and constraints that keep human potential for creativity from rising to ever higher levels.

To thrive on the edge of chaos the organization must be transformed into an organism in which deliberate planning is augmented by emergent strategies for adapting to a future that arrives unannounced.

Adapting and Planning

CHAPTER

3

Adapting and Planning

Complex systems cannot be studied by the time-honored scientific approach of breaking the system into its smallest components and studying them separately, then inferring total system behavior from the behavior of the separate parts. This scientific approach, known as reductionism, fails to consider the most important aspect of complex system behavior. This aspect is the unplanned and undirected, spontaneous interaction of the components in the process of self-organization. The interaction allows the system to adapt to a changing, uncertain, chaotic environment that cannot be fully anticipated as the future unfolds and becomes the present. Animals in nature adapt to the available supply of their food. The human immune system adapts to diseases and infections never encountered previously. The human psyche adapts to many changing conditions the likes of which could never have been anticipated. People adapted to the inhumane conditions of the concentration camps of the Holocaust and survived to tell their story to the world. Businesses adapt to changing market conditions. Adaptation is the central characteristic of complex systems that operate in part with no plan.

To adapt, we must position the system on the edge of chaos. Clusters of the system are given the authority to experiment, interact with other systems, go off on tangents, wander off course to explore what is out there, and falter many times before there is a big payoff resulting from spontaneous, breakthrough innovation. This can be achieved in a system that has balanced the unplanned with the planned responses; a system which is flexible, unplanned, and chaotic enough to permit exploration, innovation, and adaptations, together with planned responses that are steady and orderly, but not to the point of a rigidly frozen state of order. In a sense, the United States' system of government evolved this way. The states can be viewed as clusters that experiment at the local level with programs in law, health, and education that would not be prudent to test at the federal level.

Organizations Plan Too Much

There is too much planning in organizations today. The metaphors of the past 30 years are not working. Half as much planning as is presently done will be more than enough for starters. Even the nature of the planned portion will have to change if we are to embrace a model of chaos and uncertainty in system behavior as most suitable for adapting to a world characterized by chaos and uncertainty. Long-range strategic planning has seen its heyday. We must learn to bring the future closer to the present and very often respond to events in real time as they unfold. The majority, as many as two-thirds, of the organizations that have come into being in the last 10 years emerged quickly, with no long-range plan at all. They define self-organization in action. These new creations were more a result of innovative, creative thinking in which the future was brought into the present, rather than any particular planning. Obsessive planning parallels the obsession with centralized control. Both may lead to excessive rigidity with no room for adaptation.

In the course of planning, an in-depth analysis of an industry may fail you by blinding you to a future laden with low-probability, but high-impact, developments that will occur outside the industry. These developments may come from other industries, but also from the market, or the social and political environments, and may create a revolution in your own industry.

In the past 50 years, most major changes in many industries originated outside the industry. They came from people and organizations who were not customers, suppliers, allies, or competitors having a stake in the status quo. Areas seemingly unrelated to a business are the most likely source for the next major breakthrough. The computer created a revolution in word processing and the typewriter industry. Today's woman, who is not the housewife customer of the past, created a revolution for department stores. Microelectronic mechanical systems will most likely create a revolution in medical instruments and surgical procedures, and, in turn, revolutionize hospitals and health care in general. Imaging technology and computers have had their impact. There is, in all likelihood, some development somewhere, right now, that has the potential to revolutionize or permanently displace a currently thriving industry. It would be powerful for the threatened industry to bring such a future to the present whenever possible. Often, it is possible. We shall address thought processes and actions that make this possible later in the book.

Is half-planning and half-self-organizing, namely operating on the edge of chaos, compatible with the human experience? The answer is a resounding yes. If organizations operate on the edge of chaos, they will become more consistent with human nature, the mind, and the brain, by adopting the metaphor of an organism and the model of complexity theory.

Making a Half-Plan

Last summer, a friend and colleague, Robert C. Collins, M.D., Professor and Chair of the Department of Neurology at the UCLA School of Medicine, gave us a copy of his new book, *Neurology*. The book covers what we currently know about the nervous system, the brain, and the human capacity for thought, perception, language, memory, emotion, and movement. An important message repeatedly surfaced regarding the human organism, and it is the basic message of our book. The minding organization as an organism must plan for the future 50 percent, and it must be ready to respond to the 50 percent that cannot be anticipated.

In the discussion of the motor system that controls movement, Collins suggests that neural output during action depends both on past experience (the planned) and current intention (the unplanned). For example, the brain wave pattern during hand movement is unique for each movement, but there is at least 50 percent overlap across various patterns. Collins compares the human motor cortex with a piano keyboard, in which combinations of a limited number of different notes produce a rich repertoire of melodies. The piano (the planned) is augmented by spontaneous, ever-changing music (the unplanned). So also in movement, approximately one-half is unplanned, based on our encounters with a dynamic environment.

It turns out that the same is true for language. Our brains are wired to acquire a limited set of rules for understanding the language we are exposed to as children. These rules are combined with a forever-changing composition of words that produce the vast richness of language. For example, in reading the last sentence, although you have never before heard or seen the sequence of words as written above, you were able to understand the sentence. Memory is not much different. We memorize but we also improvise. The combination is rich, laden with surprises, as is evident in the theater when an actor encounters a situation that calls for a deviation from the memorized script.

I recall a scene from a play in Israel, in which a young American officer is interviewing a German conductor accused of war crimes against humanity. The scene was tense and the audience was absorbed, captivated, and swept by the historical events reenacted on stage. Suddenly, out of nowhere, there was sound of a gunshot and smoke appeared on the stage. There was shock and dead silence as the audience and the two actors froze, uncertain as to what had happened. Then we all realized that one of the lights illuminating the stage had exploded. One of the actors looked up toward the exploded bulb and quipped, "Acting is a hazardous occupation, I will ask for a raise." The audience burst out in the laughter of relief. Within a minute, the actors composed themselves. The actor portraying the American officer began, in a low and calm voice, to relate what he had experienced in the concentration camps and within a few minutes the audience was recaptured by the drama. The amazing part of all this was that the actor did not go back to the memorized script, but rather, he improvised. The movements and dialogue, his thoughts and perceptions, were all combinations of those stored in memory from before the event (the planned), with those produced in all these categories in light of the chaos that unexpectedly swept the auditorium and called for an unrehearsed, unique, unplanned response. This was creativity at its best.

It is the unrehearsed, unplanned, new movement, thought, perception, language, and emotion that is produced by human beings that is the act of creating. Movement, thought, perception, language, and emotion stored by past experiences, training, and rehearsing, can be reproduced from the planned. We can safely conclude that human experience nearly always involves both the earlier stored part, which is reproduced, and the newly created part, which is produced. The balance between the two varies. At the extreme, when we predominantly reproduce responses, there is a great deal of constancy, little surprise, and much repetition as time marches on. We have the sterility of near-perfect order. On the other hand, when we predominantly produce new, varied, and unrehearsed responses, we are constantly surprised, because we never know what will come next. We have the viability of near chaos.

On a daily basis, we should act with the balance of the planned and unplanned responses. We all have a capacity for creativity. We also have the capacity for innovation—putting new ideas, our own and those of others, to practical use. How much creativity and innovation take place depends on how much tolerance people and organizations have for the unplanned. Highly ordered and planned organizations stifle creativity and innovation. The emerging organizations that embrace the chaos and uncertainty of the unplanned thrive on creativity and innovation. Such organizations are relentless in experimenting and improvising to constantly find better and simpler ways of adapting in an interactively linked universe of systems, at times competing and at times cooperating, in their quest to survive and thrive.

Entrepreneurial organizations all start out with such seat-of-the-pants thinking and acting. Such young organizations have few rules and much vision. The goal is to carve a niche for themselves, and they actively seek new opportunities for growth. Their willingness to adapt and change is strong because they have no stake in any preconceived way of doing things. Gradually, however, as they become successful, organizational thinking loses its flexibility and becomes more fossilized. The company grows to have a stake in maintaining the status quo, with resources dedicated to its preservation. To thrive in an ever-changing world, and to keep up with entrepreneurial upstarts who would like nothing more than to replace them, organizations must reincorporate the attitude toward chaos that made them good to begin with.

As the world becomes more interconnected, planning for the future becomes more difficult. In the past, most actions in an organization were based on plans that had been devised earlier. In the present, the balance is shifting such that most actions are the result of just-in-time, unplanned decisions that emerge as unexpected events unfold and require a timely, creative response.

The tradition of long-range planning is losing its relevance. We must learn to embrace uncertainty and chaos, using flexible short-term plans that are based equally on uncertainty and chaos. A metaphor for the organizations of the past were the railroads with their fixed tracks, fixed stations for passengers to embark and disembark, fixed and closely monitored times of arrival and departure. The plan for operations was frozen, to eliminate the uncertainty of the unexpected to the extent possible. Order reigned supreme. This was the model that organizations tried to emulate in the past. The passengers of the railroad and the customers of like-minded corporations had to adapt to the plans of the respective organizations. You could go on a train any place, any time, as long as the place and time were in the plans predetermined by the railroad, just as you could later get a Ford in any color you wanted, provided you wanted black.

A metaphor for the organizations of the future is taxis cruising the roads of major cities, looking to pick up passengers. Taxis cruise in a somewhat random manner, without fixed stations, and without fixed times of arrival and departure. Uncertainty, surprise, and the unexpected are the rule. Whereas the railroads have no traffic jams (in fact, traffic is stopped to let trains go through, to ensure that the plan is not disrupted), for the taxi traffic jams are a possibility, but then the taxi can adapt and use alternate surface roads, making just-in-time decisions as events unfold on the road. The taxi has some rules of conduct—fixed pickup locations in airports and hotels, traffic lights and laws that must be obeyed, and a taxi may have arrangements with some customers for fixed and regular pickup times. Even while cruising the city streets, the route taken by a taxi is not entirely random, because it follows a path that tries to match the randomness in time and place of potential passengers. Thus, some streets will have more taxis cruising, others fewer. As demand changes because of new office buildings and hotels, or the demolition of such buildings, the number and frequency of taxis cruising the streets changes. Although the system has a communication center, scheduled maintenance, and other planned activities, it is a self-organizing system to a degree. It embraces uncertainty, chaos, and the unexpected by adapting a flexible, random plan with a repertoire of responses that attempts to match the uncertainty and chaos of the world within which it operates. The organizations of the future will embrace the metaphor of the taxi, in which uncertainty is a reality, and the need to perpetually adapt to new emerging realities is a way of life.

Organizations are finding it more difficult to identify their market, finding it less crisp and clear to define the field or business they are in as the boundaries between finance, telecommunications, health, information, commerce, and others are becoming fuzzier. There is a fusion and mingling of the fields. The distinction between partner and competitor is becoming blurred. Under such conditions, much of the planning, in particular long-range planning, is not relevant. Organizations need to start behaving like organisms, more specifically like people. Instead of creating structures and plans and then fitting people in as was the custom, we must reverse the process. We must let people tap into their inherent capacity for creativity and innovation, which is based on the unplanned and the uncertain, and let structure and plan emerge in the process. We must move from hierarchies and organizational charts to more dependence on the emergence of networks of people who are bound by links of mutual trust and respect rather than the command and control of the old order.

This new era in the life of the organization, in which the human resource is its essential and most important asset, is exciting because it frees people to do what they both enjoy and are most capable of doing. People can balance the planned with the unplanned. We use the new experiments and experiences of the unplanned to learn and change the planned. The art is to strike a balance between the two, the order and the chaos, the planned and the unplanned. Different people, different cultures, and different political systems have different predispositions to this balance. The centralized control and five-year plans of the Soviet Union left little room for the unplanned surprise of creativity and innovation; the same is true in an organization committed to excessive dependence on planning and rigid control in its execution.

People like surprise; we enjoy it and thrive on it. Humor is derived from the element of surprise. The unexpected makes the punch line funny. Here is one of the famous one-liners of comedian Henny Youngman: "I miss my wife's cooking—as often as I can." It is creativity that generates the unexpected and therefore funny second half, by twisting the meaning of the first half.

People Are the Real Assets

In the May-June 1997 issue of the *Harvard Business Review*, Norman Augustine's article ("Reshaping an Industry: Lockheed Martin's Survival Story") labels one of its subheadings "Remember That Your Real Assets Go Home at Night." He suggests that successful efforts to adapt to change depend on individuals and their collective actions, not on financial resources and corporate policies. Trust and respect are the driving forces that empower people to successfully adapt to change.

In the organization that is emerging, the real assets will not go home at night because they will not go to work in the morning; they will work wherever they are. A colleague relayed an interesting story the other day. He noticed a car parked near his office building all morning. When he left for a meeting in an adjoining building, he passed the car and realized that a friend from his school days was sitting inside. After catching up on pleasantries, the colleague asked what his friend was doing in the car all day. His friend told him that he had had an early meeting in the building across the street, and he had another meeting in the same building that afternoon, so he decided to stay in his car and work. The friend's car was fully equipped, like an office, and with all the travel demanded of his job, it made more sense to work from his car than from a rented office in a stationary building.

The revolution of the wired world is upon us. It calls for adaptation to a life at the edge of chaos. It calls for a new model of the organization. This model is the science of the twenty-first century and is rooted in the theory of chaos, a theory that reveals the hidden, underlying order that is not apparent in complex systems. Even as taxis cruise the streets in what appears to be random, chaotic fashion, there is an underlying order in the system. As we noted earlier, complex systems such as neurons in the human brain and organizations in a global market cannot be studied using the traditional scientific method of breaking the system apart, analyzing the components, and using the findings to infer the behavior of the entire system. It does not work because the system behavior is unplanned and not directed. In fact, it springs from spontaneous interactions among the components, which is what we call *self-organizing*.

Self-Organization Sparks Creativity

One attribute of self-organizing systems is adaptation. The brain adapts to inputs from the environment, the body adapts to infection and injury, and organizations adapt to changing realities and market conditions.

A second attribute of complex self-organizing systems is more amazing and illuminating. It appears that complex systems tend to position themselves at the boundary between operating in a stable fashion, based on a set plan, and at the same time responding with creativity and innovation to unplanned, unrehearsed, and unexpected developments that call for change, flexibility, and risk. This boundary is the edge of chaos. Moving too far away from this edge toward the planned and stable, the system freezes and becomes sterile; moving too far toward the unplanned, the system collapses in chaos and disarray.

A third attribute of complex self-organizing systems has a most profound effect on the likelihood for adaptation on the edge of chaos. This is the size of the system, and the amount of diversity within it. Innovation occurs best in small groups of diverse backgrounds. Uniformity and sameness, with no intellectual and cultural diversity, stifle innovation. With our increasing reliance on "global togetherness" through cyberspace and mass media, many individual differences may disappear; the implications for creativity, adaptation, and innovation may be deadly.

The question is whether we can spark ideas to help use cyberspace in ways that will enhance creativity, innovation, and adaptation. At present, we appear to have no explicit road map, no plan. However, the brain is capable of dealing with a panorama of complex terrain, with no roads or sense of direction, let alone a road map. If we have an attractor in the form of a purpose, we shall adapt.

Structure, Creativity, and Error

THE FOUNDATIONS OF THE MINDING ORGANIZATION

Structure, Creativity, and Error

THE FOUNDATIONS OF THE MINDING ORGANIZATION

Hierarchies and Networks

Organizations come into being with creativity and innovation, sparked by a network of people who have a shared sense of purpose. They self-organize with no rules or procedures codified in a manual. There is neither a manual, nor is there any organizational hierarchy; everything is loose, evolving, and in a state of flux. As the young organization grows and learns from experience what worked and what did not work, it begins to codify and institutionalize rules and procedures to guide people to do in the future what worked in the past. With this comes the assignment of authority, responsibility, and status to enforce the rules. This is the beginning of hierarchical structure. Entrepreneurial conduct is displaced by bureaucratic structure, which stifles creativity. Now, people have to bend the rules or go around the rules to find a network of supporters, collaborators, and champions of ideas, who are in many different places in the hierarchy. A process of evoking new networks begins to take place. Authority, responsibility, status, and compensation are not the criteria for centrality or key positions in the network. A key position might be held by the person who makes the appointments for the chief financial officer. By being linked to such a key person, you might get the timely appointment that opens the door to engaging a champion to support your new idea.

Recently, a high school classmate of mine, a physician who is an accomplished cancer researcher, related an experience that illustrates how a gatekeeper can make or break ideas for change. My friend had just finished medical school in Europe, at a university with a rigid hierarchical structure. She then wanted to explore a research idea that she had once discussed with one of her professors, a leading cancer researcher in Europe. She worked in his laboratory during the final summer of her studies and tried several times to get an appointment with him. Each time, she was turned away by the gatekeeper at his office. My friend took a position with another reputable research lab elsewhere in Europe. Years later the professor, whom she did not get to see, told her that he had been disappointed that she had left his lab to work elsewhere. He had waited for her, and he was hurt to learn that she had left. So much for how high in the hierarchy you are, and how easy it is to sabotage at lower levels. The informal network in the organization can promote change or stifle it; it can augment or disrupt the structure that the hierarchy is attempting to create. Hierarchies are formal, explicit, rigid, guided by rules of a manual, and bound by authority. Hierarchies are like trains moving on fixed tracks, making stops based on predetermined plans. Networks are informal, implicit, flexible, guided by rules of thumb, and bound by mutual trust. Networks are like taxis cruising the city, moving randomly through surface streets and making stops that are mostly unplanned.

We need both hierarchies and networks. Networks are more prevalent early, in the creative and innovative stages of a new undertaking, whereas hierarchies are more prevalent and useful when ideas are to be implemented in the marketplace. A thriving, growing, renewing organization is one that learns to operate on the edge of chaos. Such an organization learns to maintain the delicate shifting balance between hierarchies and networks, the deliberately planned and the emerging, surprising, unplanned responses to a world marked by chaos and uncertainty.

Creative Tension

Organizations, by their very nature, require structure, order, and rules to function. This is contrary to the environment necessary to tap into human creativity. Chaos, flexibility, and looser frameworks are the requisite characteristics for developing fresh ideas and novel plans. Unconventional ideas cannot be fostered in conventional organizations that are dominated by excessive structure. There is, then, a need for a new balance within organizations, which will nurture the creative thinking necessary for the organization's survival, together with a framework that can respond to the more mundane, daily needs of the organization, which depend on structure and order.

Organizations must find a way to oscillate between chaos and order, a process that fosters creative thinking. Just as excessive order can stifle creativity, excessive chaos has its own pitfalls. Without closure to ideas, without a structure that can deliver a finished product, creative ideas float without direction. At some stage, the product must reach a customer who will have little or no knowledge about the creative process that fostered the development of the product but who will know when and where they want the product delivered. This aspect of organization demands structure and order, a bureaucracy that is responsible for the skeletal workings of the organizations. Unfortunately, most organizations devote the bulk of their efforts to the skeletal workings, and very little effort to the real heart of their enterprise, the part involving creative thinking.

Essentially then, we have two extremes: excessive structure, which stifles creativity, and excessive chaos, which may produce individual creativity but never produce the goods. This dichotomy results in mental creative tension most strongly felt by those within the organization who want to innovate. This tension can be used advantageously by taking individual creative inputs from a chaotic state into a more structured and orderly state, finding a way to materialize the innovative thinking into an organization's structure.

Creativity demands a certain push, pull, and shove to take off. Our current business environments and systems do anything but encourage the plunge into creativity. Executives have short-term commitments from employers; this fosters critical-thinking analysis, logic, and the search for quick solutions. How then to get employees thinking creatively? This demands trust, which a short-term commitment does not foster.

In the minding organization, creativity is neither delegated to a certain division within the corporate structure, nor is it designated as a function of certain management levels, nor is it tucked away in R&D. Creativity becomes the corporate culture; it is nurtured, encouraged, and rewarded at all levels, especially at the front lines, on the assembly line floor, at the receptionist's desk—wherever business makes contact with the client. Such a culture requires an ingredient lacking in all but a few management circles: trust. Trusting that the people in the organization have the best interests of the organization at heart, trusting their judgment, and allowing everyone in the organization the authority to experiment and make mistakes in their attempt to innovate and create.

These elements of trust require a particular environment. Trusting judgment requires that you carefully choose whom you recruit and hire into the organization. Ensuring that all involved have the best interest of the organization in their minds requires an environment that puts the best interest of the organization and the best interests of the individuals on the same plane. The authority to make mistakes is probably the most important of all of these, and it is crucial to the future success of a business. The underlying axiom will be that we give individuals the responsibility to be right but also the authority to be wrong. Once we free our perceptions of error as negative forces, we can allow ourselves the latitude to foster creativity.

The Pac-Man Story

When you glance at Figure 4.1, what does it look like? A pie with a piece removed? A part of a circle? A "Pac-Man" perhaps? A generation ago, nobody would have said Pac-Man, but the world is changing rapidly, and one of the figures we now have all had some exposure to is the Pac-Man.

Now, look at Figure 4.2. There are four Pac-Men. Are they an organization? They certainly do not look like they are coordinating their efforts toward any common goal. They look more like a random collection of Pac-Men.

How about Figure 4.3? Here, they are closer together, but they all seem to have their backs to one another and do not look like they are on speaking terms. If someone were to walk into this type of organization, what would they think? Is this an organization with which you want to do business?

What about Figure 4.4? The Pac-Men are now aligned at least, and we can discern structure, but they are all doing exactly the same thing. How much added value does each Pac-Man contribute to the whole? Does this seem like an interesting state-of-the-art organization? Does this structure create a vital, thriving organization?

FIGURE 4.1 Single Pac-Man.

FIGURE 4.2 Four jumbled Pac-Men.

Now, take a look at the next configuration of Pac-Men in Figure 4.5. What figure immediately jumps to the forefront? The Pac-Men appear to form a square. The amazing aspect of their coordinated effort is the creation of a new entity, which in reality does not even exist—if you cover the Pac-Men with your hands, there will be no square. We see lines connecting the Pac-Men, despite the fact that there are no lines on the paper. The image is so forceful that the square appears to be brighter than the surrounding context, when in fact, even this is not so. What we perceive with respect to the square exists solely in our brains, and it is the result of our tremendous perceptual capabilities. Imagine yourself as the customer coming into this organization. The organization has created a structure that causes you to perceive a square. Thus, their efforts are toward your perceptions, and perceptions are the force of the future.

The appearance of the square depends on the effort of each individual Pac-Man; each must coordinate its efforts with the

FIGURE 4.3 Four differently arranged Pac-Men.

FIGURE 4.4 Four aligned Pac-Men.

two adjacent Pac-Men. The Pac-Men are able to create squares of various sizes; essentially, they can create custom-sized squares to fit the demands of individual customers, but they can only do so if they work as a team. Likewise, there are limits and constraints on their productivity. If they move too far away from each other, the image of a square will disappear from sight. The structure of the team is the critical determinant of the success in this organization. We see, therefore, that the choice of internal structure determines the type of creative ideas the organization is able to produce. The structure must be flexible enough to maximize the contribution of each individual within the organization.

The efforts of the four-Pac-Men team have resulted in a creative grouping, taking chaos and transforming it to order. Were these Pac-Men to cease additional efforts, the competition would not only leave them all in a trail of dust, but the team

FIGURE 4.5 Four Pac-Men in corners.

members themselves would soon grow frustrated at having to continue the same work. Once the creative effort is institutionalized, it becomes stale and mindless. If the organization wants to continue making squares, there will have to be a way to allow the team members to pursue new creative endeavors as well. Both the organization and the individuals have everything to gain from an environment dedicated to individual and team productivity.

Heightened Perception

The Pac-Man example brings our focus to the next frontier for the human brain. With computer technologies taking over information processing and logical operations, the human brain must now move forward and upward by going back to what we humans do best—perceive acutely. Our powers of perception, our ability to enrich the potential meaning of information channeled through our senses, applying greater depth and breadth to the way we look and see, hear and listen, allows us to improve the quality and quantity of our ideas, thoughts, and actions.

The art of improvising depends on our skills of perception. In an unfamiliar situation, faced with unexpected obstacles, the human brain is able to extract information and impose meaning in previously inexperienced ways. Our thinking is stimulated by having a rich and flexible repertoire of viewpoints. A rigid perception acts as a filter, not only rejecting ideas that do not fit the model, but blocking the mind from creating ideas through alternative perceptions. One of the most fertile grounds for developing alternative perceptions is conversation. The word *conversation* contains the root of the word for opposite, *converse*. It comes from the Latin for *turning around together*. This is the essence of a conversation. Opposite views are articulated, and in the process, new insights are gained. To truly benefit from a conversation, we must enter the process with a readiness to listen and comprehend the perceptions of others, to understand their frame of reference regardless of how remote these are from our own perceptions. To comprehend another point of view does not mean to accept it as superior to one's own point of view. Mature, clear thinking is taking the time to give a new perception a chance to be tested. Much of the time we spend speaking with other people does not qualify as conversation, but rather, as an opportunity to vocalize and listen to ourselves, or to exchange information, but not share frames of mind.

A minding organization must not only be cognizant of the perceptions within, but must also monitor the perceptions of its customers on an ongoing basis. Customers have perceptions about organizations as well as about the products and services they provide. The first contact a customer has with an organization creates an image that may last a lifetime. An organization cannot assume that the image they try to portray is the image perceived by the customer.

Perceptions must be relentlessly monitored. A minding organization, as a viable organism, must document and store ever-changing perceptions and frames of reference as part of the organization's memory. Assuming that the customer of five years ago is still the customer of today will quickly outdate an organization. Companies that were very successful manufacturing typewriters knew that improvements in their machines would be well received and appreciated by the typing public and that new models would be bought quickly. Are those typing customers still out there? Those same customers have turned to a completely new technology, and no new improvement in typewriters will bring them back. Typewriters are now perceived as a tool of a past generation. Typewriter manufacturers needed to be aware of changing perceptions, and assimilate such changes as quickly as possible, as should any organization that deals with a customer. This requires more than lip service, as the Big Three American automakers learned in the 1970s.

Every individual is a filter for perceiving the world. People carve out portions of reality that fit the frame from which they view the world, but they assume that they are processing reality in its entirety. Once in a while, we are shaken to realize that others see things so differently from ourselves that we cannot help but understand that our frameworks are limited; most of the time our awareness is what is limited. We think and act as though everyone shares our frame of reference, when in fact, each person's framework carves out a unique portion of reality. On a tour bus in a foreign city, every person on the bus will end the tour with a different perception of the city. An architect will note the building styles; a gardener will focus on the landscape and plant forms; the fashion-conscious person will perceive what people are wearing, and so on. Although you may notice absolutely none of these things, all are within everyone's line of vision, but are not within everyone's frame of reference.

In an organization, with so many specialties and so much fragmentation of manual work and brain work, each person looks at a situation through different filters. Unless a way is found to reconcile these differences in frames, misunderstanding and lack of communication will be a driving force, tearing away at the potential for creativity. The only way to reconcile differences in frames of reference is for each person in the organization to be both a generalist and a specialist.

An individual working within a fragmented organization will have to know a little about the other fragments, at the boundaries of the specialty, creating a generalist, reflecting the entire organization. A specialty will be shared at a general level with others in the organization so that each worker will have some level of knowledge of any specialty linked or adjacent to his specialty. Specialists will have the most detail, but everyone within the organization will have some level of understanding, which will provide a frame of reference uniting the entire organization. To reframe, then, means to frame again and again, adding additional frames to a growing repertoire of perceptual abilities.

In teamwork, the ability to share each other's frames is the foundation for the team's ability to realize a shared goal. Sharing frames does not mean choosing one frame as best, or judging frames relative to each other. The key to effective teamwork is balance, reconciling opposing frames of reference in a way that serves the goal. Even in this concept, there are multiple ways of viewing the situation. For example, the word *compromise* connotes that each person has to give up something for the common good. The frame of mind raised by *compromise* has little gain for the individuals involved; each just tries to give up as little as possible. If, instead, the focus is on *balance* and *reconciling*, the frame is much more positive. With *compromise*, nobody gets their way; with *balance*, the result is "our" way, which is more than each of the individual ways.

In a team, each person comes with the filter of their specialty (manufacturing, marketing, maintenance, finance, law), but he or she must become a generalist in the field of their team members. Otherwise, communication is impossible, and output is meager. To become greater than the sum of the parts, team members must put away the attitude of "that's not my problem" and adopt the problems of the entire team as their own. Certain team members may be more specialized at particular aspects of a problem, but all team members must be minding the problem. Framing, then, must be both in terms of individuals and in terms of teams.

What We Look For and What We See

To heighten our perceptual abilities, we need to first break down the skills involved. Perception involves a combination of what our senses take in together with a choice we make of where to put our attention. For example, looking and listening are deliberate choices. I can choose to look up or down; I can choose to listen to one speaker or another. What we see and hear depends on what we have chosen to attend to, and what meaning we impose on the information. At the conceptual level, we can look at a situation from different points of view and see different issues come to light. For example, in designing new products, looking at manufacturing issues brings different visions than those that are stimulated by looking at maintenance. Manufacturing may elicit visions of easy ways of putting parts together, whereas maintenance focuses on easy ways to take things apart. The two ways may not be congruent, nor even compatible, in a design.

The more flexible and rich our repertoire of ways of looking, the more fertile is the domain of what we see, and the more stimulated is our thinking. Flexibility and richness in how we look can reduce the potential for errors of omission and errors of commission that attend a fixed way of looking with a rigid perception. A rigid perception acts as a filter. The filter rejects that which does not fit the model and accepts only that which does fit.

Look at the sequence of the three symbols in Figure 4.6. You see the middle symbol as the letter B because you are looking at it in the context of letters. You accept the parts that fit a B in your perceptual model of a B and reject whatever does not fit.

Now, look at the sequence of the three symbols in Figure 4.7. You now see the middle symbol as the digit 8 because the sequence suggests that you are looking at numbers, and if you choose to look at the middle symbol as a number, you will see an 8 by rejecting and accepting whatever it takes to make it fit your model of an 8.

To an extent, when a problem is well formulated it is virtually solved. Finding the appropriate way of looking at a problem is a very important phase in the creative process. As a simple example, consider the following sequence: 213 475 6198. You most likely see it as a telephone number because it looks like one. Now, look at this sequence: 821 347 5619. If you dismiss it as only another telephone number, you are too rigid in your looking. It could be a license plate of an automobile (possibly a foreign car), but in addition, if you inspect the two sequences

FIGURE 4.6 A-B-C.

FIGURE 4.7 7-8-9.

and look for relations, you will note something. Can you guess the next 10 sequences?

Old Woman, Young Woman, and More on the Same Frame

Consider Figure 4.8. Normally, people can see an old woman and a young woman in the figure. Through heightened perception, however, you can see much more. Again, what you see is determined by what you choose to look for. What you look for becomes a mental picture that acts as a filter. We filter details that do not fit the mental picture and admit the details that fit. Often, this mental picture will filter (ignore) aspects of a part that do not fit but accept other aspects of that part that are congruent with the mental picture. Note that the part of the figure that you see as an eye when you look for an old woman, you see as an ear when you look for the young woman. What the symbol or detail means depends on the context, the mental picture, the perception.

Inspect the figure and look for different pictures by focusing on different parts of the figure, turning it sideways, upside down, or blocking the two faces out and concentrating on what is left. Be flexible. Information is sterile until it takes on meaning. Meaning is imposed by observers depending on their perceptions. Computers process information. Humans process meaning in addition to information. To understand the point of view of another person is to be able to see the way that person perceives the world, and thus impose the same meaning on what becomes then a shared experience.

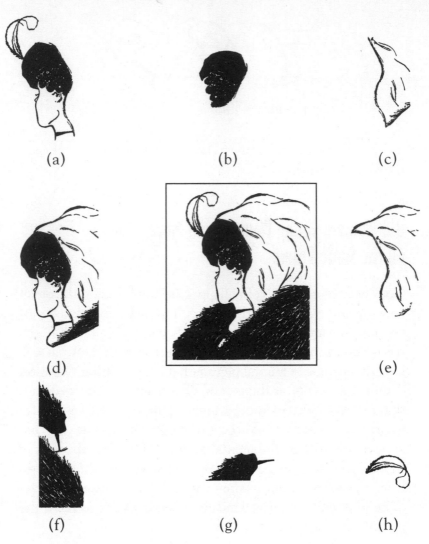

(a)   (b)   (c)

(d)   (e)

(f)   (g)   (h)

FIGURE 4.8 Young woman/old woman—a matter of perception.

In the old woman and young woman figure, we can see a great deal more than two women. A woman in a seminar once jumped with excitement and said she saw a man in the figure. When asked how she could see a man when we had two women, she said "because I have been looking for one," then added jokingly "for a long time." Can you see the man? Who does he look like? Inspect the nine figures around the center figure in the box and describe what you perceive.

Good or Bad? A Question of Perception and Context

We paraphrase Shakespeare's famous quote from Hamlet: Nothing is good or bad, but perception makes it so. Everything is in the eyes of the beholder, depending on how we choose to behold. How we frame an observation or an experience can make it appear good or bad, depending on the context or the perception imposed. The perception can act as a filter to omit what does not fit and commit what fits the perception. Consider the 3M Post-it Pads. When the glue was first tried, it was considered a failure because the perception was that the glue should be used for a strong connection; we normally glue things so they stay firmly together. It was only when the perception was changed to situations requiring weak connections (such as marking pages in a book for reference) that the glue, which appeared to be a failure in one context, became a remarkable success in a new context. The weak glue in the context of strong, durable connections became very good glue for temporary and reusable connections.

Our perceptions are models. We accept what fits the model, and we reject that which does not fit. On the one hand, we need stable models to make sense of the world; on the other hand, we need flexibility to change the models so we can continue to learn and adapt to a changing world. Stability and flexibility appear to be in conflict. The more we have of one attribute the less we have of the other. At the extremes, we have stability with rigidity, order, and no adaptability at one end, and flexibility and chaos with no stability at the other. Either extreme does not answer the need for stable, predictable models of behavior that have a built-in flexibility to adapt to change. We must seek a balance between stability and flexibility. The more we learn and the more we know, the more filters we create that block the admissibility of new information that does not fit what we know. The inadmissible new information could bring about new knowledge if admitted; namely, it could refine our filters.

The Expert as Filter

The expert opinion in every field constitutes a filter. It is a highly focused perception, a tunnel vision, not a panoramic view of the situation. We need filtered information because our limited rationality cannot encompass the complexity of the world in its raw, unfiltered fashion. Filters reduce the amount of detail we must process and, thus, make the complex simple enough for us to comprehend. However, every time we use a filter, we discard a part of the total picture. We perceive different pictures through different filters. To use one rigid model as a filter is very limiting; to do so without being aware of the implications of such rigid perception can block all learning. We must be sensitive to the biases and limitations of the models we use to filter information. In summary, we cannot separate observers and their filters from what is being observed. Being aware of this is the first step toward a process that may balance the stability of constancy with the flexibility of adaptability, a balance that is necessary if we are to continue learning and improving in a changing environment. We need a model to strive for balance between order and chaos, between structure and creativity.

Strategies to Enhance Creativity in Organizations

There are several strategies that will enhance creativity and innovation and contribute to the emergence of a minding organization.

DIVERSITY

Creativity thrives on diversity. Teams, working on projects requiring creativity, should comprise individuals spanning a wide range of diverse interests, specialties, cultures, and talents. The more diverse the group, the richer and wider-ranging will be the conversations, and the more fertile the field for yielding creative ideas. Studies have shown that diverse groups take longer to get started, but they end up with much higher levels of creative and innovative ideas than homogeneous groups. Homogeneous groups are more potent, effective, and quick to implement ideas and plans requiring habitual thinking. Heterogeneous, diverse groups are more powerful with the unplanned issues that require spontaneous thinking. These findings provide a strategy for organizations to create or plan an environment for both homogeneous and heterogeneous networks to emerge.

OPPOSITES

Embrace early on the full spectrum of opposites on the scales of issues, attributes, and measurement. For example, view positive and negative aspects of an issue. Consider a competitor as a potential ally, and consider an ally as a potential competitor. Consider a compliment whenever you have a reprimand in mind; perhaps you will use both. Opposites, conflicts, dichotomies, and paradoxes kept simultaneously in mind tend to trigger ideas that break out of the bondage of old contexts and create surprisingly new ideas. By embracing opposites, the familiar is made strange and the strange becomes familiar. In the book of Genesis, a day emerged as the context for the coexistence of darkness and light. Einstein created a context for motion and rest to coexist. A man standing on an escalator is moving with respect to a person standing on the ground, but is at rest with respect to a person standing next to him on the escalator. Thus, the concept of relativity was born. Dirac's concept of antimatter is defined by particles opposite in electric charge to all other known particles. The concept of antimatter provided an explanation of strange phenomena that could not be explained by existing theories.

Consider a house that was on the market for many months with no potential buyer in sight. When the house was considered in terms of opposites—value and disvalue—a new idea was born. The original context was a residential community that places high value on single-family dwellings. The context for disvalue was imagined as a house fit for a residential area, located on land that was earmarked for commercial development. Such land would be more valuable with no house on it. The house would thus represent disvalue. A study of trends suggested a potential for rezoning of the neighborhood. Within a year the land was put up for sale, ignoring the value of the house. It was sold within weeks for four times the asking price compared with the previous attempt to sell the house with the land in the context of property in a residential neighborhood.

SHARING KNOWLEDGE: THE GLOBAL ORGANIZATION NETWORK

Over the last 50 years, change in almost every industry has come from outside, mostly from noncustomers and industries who were never considered to be competitors. We must find ways to create a web of relationships among diverse, noncompetitive organizations that are dedicated to mutual support and bound by mutual trust. Five to nine such organizations that are part of a cluster within such a web could provide each other an objective, legitimate, supportive, and risk-free sounding board in an environment of total amnesty. There would be no fear to share and explore ideas for what the future holds. Clusters could be linked in a global network with hubs in major universities. Member organizations would help each other on a reciprocal basis, at no charge, enhancing the potential for creativity, innovation, and success in business applications. The breadth and diversity of such a web of a global corporate network would achieve a kind of coevolution for member organizations.

A five-day program on creativity and innovation in the organization now exists at UCLA. The program introduces the thought processes and the models, and sets the stage for the agenda of the future and membership in the global web of the corporate network. Quarterly one-day meetings of clusters at member sites and at university hubs are augmented by special sessions convened by cluster members to use others as a sounding board for special urgent issues that emerge (the unplanned). University hubs keep the different clusters linked, using the tools of telecommunications and face-to-face sessions as needed to keep the network viable.

In special situations, executives of member organizations trade places from time to time to learn from each other. This exchange is augmented by exchange at other levels of work within an organization. Becoming a part of such a network helps member organizations achieve the following:

- Leverage wisdom, knowledge, and skills
- Leverage corporate resources, both human and financial
- Provide early detection and awareness of trends
- Promote self-renewal on a timely basis
- Form business alliances and partnerships
- Provide an unbiased arena to experiment with new ideas
- Visit the future

Articulating Errors

The Hebrew word for *sin* is derived from the root of a word that means "missing the target." If to sin is to miss the target, then to err is no more than target practice before the real contest takes place. Errors and mistakes are, indeed, target practice and continued experimentation in the quest for improvement. To learn from errors is imperative if we are committed to continued learning. Experience is not only to know what will work in a particular situation, but also to know what will not work. Errors provide the most profound opportunity to foster an environment of total amnesty, in which trust and mutual respect drive out the fear of mistakes and permit quick experimentation with ideas in which all involved continue to learn.

MOSHE'S STORY: CREATING A LEARNING ENVIRONMENT OF TOTAL AMNESTY

When I was a student, I was awed by the flawless performance of some of my teachers. When on some occasion a teacher made an error on the blackboard and could not explain what went wrong, the teacher would be visibly flustered. I shared the teacher's embarrassment, but not everybody did. Some students were visibly delighted. They enjoyed an opportunity to get even, as if thinking, "You, teacher, catch us when we err, now we caught you!"

When I started my academic career more than 30 years ago, I dreaded the thought of finding myself in such an embarrassing situation. I prepared carefully for each lecture. I wrote out most of what I had to say on yellow pads, and derived every equation before doing it in class. I took special pride when, in the process of extensive preparation, I could derive on the blackboard a result involving many steps without resorting to the prepared notes. I could sense on such occasions the students' awe, and possible intimidation, as they raced to copy what I had derived on the blackboard from memory without the aid of notes. However, I was very tense before and during the lectures. I was too concerned (consciously or subconsciously) with the fear of failure, fear of mistakes, fear of questions for which I would have no satisfactory answers, or no answers at all. The tension was so great that, at times, I questioned whether teaching was the right profession for me.

Despite all my preparations, there were embarrassing moments with errors that I made and questions that I answered in a less-than-satisfactory manner. I managed to recover from these embarrassing situations and I even improved with time, but I could not eliminate all potential errors. My frustration persisted. Then came the opportunity for a paradigm shift. When the system that had worked thus far—namely, finding ways to avoid errors, and when I could not, working around them or trying to hide the fact that I was lost—broke down, I made a shift in attitude that changed my life as an educator. When a system breaks down, it is an opportunity for change. Here is my story and its aftermath.

I had just completed a mathematical derivation that required a lengthy development covering two blackboards in the front of the room and one board on the side wall. A student raised his hand and asked a question about the derivation. There was a contradiction, he claimed, between what I set out to derive and what I finally derived. A quick look at the result convinced me that something was wrong. But what? I looked at my notes. The same result appeared there. My notes must be wrong, too, I thought. Where was the error? I was lost. I began to perspire; I scanned the blackboard for a hint of where I went wrong, but found no clue. My panic must have been apparent, because the class of some 40 graduate students came to life at 8:30 P.M., one-half hour before the class was to be over. Even the students who were half asleep most of the semester woke up and offered advice. I was so embarrassed that I hoped for a hidden hatch to open in the floor to swallow me. The class took over; everyone was talking. Two students stood up, pointing to various equations and offering advice as to what might be wrong on the blackboard. Other students gave advice from their seats. A spontaneous thought came to my rescue and I made a quick decision. "Class," I said in a loud voice, "do you know what is a teacher's best friend?" The room fell silent, with all eyes on me. I walked over to the blackboard, took two erasers, one in each hand, and quickly erased what was written on the three blackboards. Then holding up an eraser I said: "This is the teacher's best friend." I then told the class that I was very embarrassed, I had made an error, I was lost and confused, and there was no point in wasting the remaining 20 minutes of class time. I suggested that we end the class early, go home to try to unravel what went wrong, and discuss it next time. My tension subsided and I even felt relaxed. I had done it. I had told the class the simple truth that I had made an error and that I did not know how to correct it.

ENCOURAGE ERRORS

From the day of that incident I changed. The environment in my classes changed. Fear of error gave way to commitment to learning by all, teacher and students alike. I discuss my philosophy of teaching and learning with each new group. Errors are not a problem; rather, it is our attitude to errors that matters. We must begin by encouraging errors. Yes, encouraging errors. Whenever we attempt to learn something new, or try to do something new, we must experiment. We can only learn when we are free of the fear of failure. Even at more advanced stages of knowledge, we must be tolerant of errors. Errors are part of the human experience. If we make more errors in the early stages of learning, we make fewer errors later on, and we become more adept at detecting and correcting them without our egos getting too much in the way. There is more maturity displayed by a positive attitude toward errors—our own and those of others—than by the arrogance of perfect knowledge.

CELEBRATE FAILURE

Learning is a function of trial and error. *To err* comes from the Latin, *errare*, meaning to wander off course, not in the wrong direction, but in a different direction from the anticipated path. In the process of erring, phenomenal discoveries may be unearthed. Wisdom is the collection of experiences that teaches us not only what will work, but also what will not work. A healthy attitude toward error is a lucrative asset that creates a mind open to new opportunities. An error is a gap between what was anticipated and what actually resulted. The gap can be negative, so that the results are less than what was anticipated. The gap can just as easily be positive, so that the results are more than what was anticipated. Either way, the difference must be thought through to maximize benefits by learning from what went wrong as well as what went right.

If the gap is negative, clearly you would like to avoid such gaps in the future. Covering up or dismissing such errors as aberrations is probably the world's most common, but worst, way of handling failure. The only way to decrease the likelihood of negative gaps is to understand what caused them in the first place.

When the gaps are positive, they are celebrated but rarely investigated. Getting more than you anticipated is wonderful for the ego, and people love to attribute such success to their inherent abilities. Once again, the disparity between what was anticipated and what resulted ought to be given serious thought, in this case, to ensure that future success is more likely.

One way to foster a healthy attitude toward error is to treat failures the same way we treat success. We ought to celebrate failures! Our Western culture is partially responsible for the way most of us treat errors as negative forces to be ignored or challenged. Ask a room full of people how many of them like to be wrong, and very few hands will go up. The typical error scenario is that we either keep our mistake quiet and hope nobody will notice, or if an error is publicized, we make every effort to attribute a mistake to a source outside ourselves. We recall an amusing case of a colleague studying from a math textbook that provided answers to selected problems at the end of the text. This man calculated an answer that computed differently from the answer at the back of the book. Instead of trying to see where he might have gone wrong, he spent the next several hours trying to determine why the book was wrong!

In other cultures that are less results-oriented than ourselves, the attitude toward error is less severe. Does this really mean that we ought to celebrate failures? It would be difficult to imagine a world in which we awake each morning, cheerfully thinking about how many different ways we can possibly do things wrong today, but this would take an attitude to error to the other extreme. We need not focus on the extremes; there are other options. What if an organization gave people the authority to be wrong, and cemented the relationship by celebrating the error of the week? Individuals would be waiting in line to work in such an environment.

This is not an attitude of "feel good, set no standards." Some educators today feel that self-esteem is more important than learning; thus, they do not create challenges, to avoid failures. The attitude we are advocating is to embrace failures willingly and learn from them, turning unanticipated outcomes into opportunities.

Children need to make their own mistakes to achieve maturity; an organization should also be allowed to learn from its own mistakes. Just as the child must try and err to establish an identity, so must an organization challenge itself and learn from resulting gaps to identify itself. Every single person associated with the organization must be given the responsibility for learning. This is tantamount to declaring that every single person in an organization must be given the responsibility to be right but also the authority to be wrong. It is only in such an environment that gaps will be evaluated, whether they are positive or negative. No type of gap will be ignored nor dismissed, touted nor celebrated, without gaining new insights and understanding. Insight and understanding can be brought to a new dimension of "innerstanding" by choosing to focus on what went wrong as well as what went right.

Articulation of errors, then, has tremendous growth potential. To ignore gaps is to stagnate; to mark gaps (celebrating the positive and reframing the negative into possible avenues to develop) is to take complete charge of a maturing self. This is as true for individuals personally as it is true for individuals in an organization.

What happens if you are the best in your field? Are there any errors to articulate? Of course! The concept of error as a gap between performance and intention is connected with the notion of benchmarking. If you provide a service or product, in any industry, you constantly have your eye on what characterizes the best in your field. The company that provides the service most valued by consumers at a competitive price with reasonable costs is considered the industry best, and hence the benchmark with which you compare yourself. Each wants to be the industry benchmark on at least some characteristic. Suppose you reach the goal of becoming the benchmark and you are number one in your field. With what do you now compare yourself? You compare yourself with your own previous performance.

Error, then, must be articulated, comprehended, related to past experience, and made part of the organization's memory. People learn more when something goes wrong than when everything goes right. If there is one way to do something right, there are hundreds of ways to do it wrong. Refusing to recognize that errors are important to articulate is the single most damaging error one can make.

Errors as a Source of Innovation

Numerous successful products were a result of the unplanned. Errors generate information that can be put to productive use, if only our minds are open to the possibilities.

TEA BAGS

Thomas Sullivan, a tea merchant, often sent samples of tea packed in cans to his customers. In 1904, Sullivan decided it would be easier and cheaper to send the tea samples in small silk bags. Soon orders began arriving, specifically for the tea packaged in the bags! Customers had discovered that brewing the tea in the small bags made the process easier.

PENICILLIN

Alexander Fleming, a bacteriologist, arrived at his research lab one day in September 1928, and found that he had left one of his experimental plates containing the staphylococci bacteria near an open window. When he looked at the plate, he saw that some mold had come through the window and contaminated the bacteria. Others might have thought the experiment spoiled, thrown away the plate, and started over. Fleming, however, investigated the error, and found under his microscope that although mold covered the bacteria, around the mold there was a clear zone. The deadly bacteria were being dissolved by the mold. Articulation of the error gave the world penicillin.

POST-IT NOTES

Post-it Notes were not a planned product. No one got the idea and stayed up nights to invent it. Spencer Silver was working in the 3M research labs in 1970 trying to find a strong adhesive. The adhesive Silver developed was even weaker than what 3M already produced. It stuck to objects, but could easily be lifted off. It was superweak instead of superstrong—a failure in the mind-set of the inventor. Four years later, another 3M scientist, Arthur Fry, was singing in his church choir. He used markers to keep his place in the hymnal, but they kept falling out of the book. Remembering Silver's adhesive, Fry worked to develop a machine that could produce pads of paper. This was no small feat, as 3M was only geared to produce products in rolls. 3M began distributing Post-it Notes in 1980, but the initial sales were so disappointing that 3M executives wanted to stop production. Fry insisted that customers be interviewed, to understand the gap between the success 3M had expected and the poor sales that resulted. They learned that customers who actually used the product loved it and wanted to buy more, but sales were low because most people did not know what the product was. 3M decided to give away thousands of samples to teach people about the product, which subsequently has become a staple in every home and office.

SCOTCHGARD

Scotchgard is the brand name of a fabric protector. In the 1950s, researchers at 3M were testing fluorochemicals for use on aircraft. Some of the chemical spilled on a researcher's tennis shoe. As time went on, she noticed that as her tennis shoes got dirty from wear, one area remained clean. She recognized this as the spot that had been touched by the chemical. Scotchgard was the outcome of an error and heightened perception.

BRAILLE

Successful innovations are often the result of several generations of product improvements, each successive generation a result of lessons learned from the previous cycle. Several hundred years after the invention of the printing press, a French professor of calligraphy thought that the blind might be able to read with their fingers. Valentin Hauy devised an italic typeface of the alphabet and had it embossed in raised letters. At the end of each line, the hand had to be moved back to the left of the page without losing track of its position. James Frere's contribution was to think up the return line, which meant printing lines alternately, one from left to right and the next from right to left. Both Hauy and Frere were sighted; it took the ingenuity of an actual user of the system, a customer, to perfect the system.

Louis Braille had been accidentally blinded in one eye at the age of three. Within a few years, sympathetic ophthalmia blinded his other eye. Braille, an avid learner, found the Hauy method lacking. He turned to a system called night writing, which allowed French soldiers to communicate in the dark. The system used 12 raised dots, grouped in different ways to represent the alphabet. Braille simplified the code to 6 dots with easier groupings. In 1825, the 16-year-old Braille presented his new system. School authorities were slow to accept Braille's method, claiming that Braille was too young to really understand the problem. Also, they considered his system too simple. It would take more than 50 years for his system to be widely recognized as superior, because the decisions were made by sighted people who could not comprehend the frustrations of the blind.

Errors as Organizational Strategy

The attitude toward errors and the articulation of errors are central elements in the creative process. Creative people handle errors in a way that enhances the creative process. Most people performing a difficult task tend to be careful, controlled, and wary of making errors. Creative people have the opposite predisposition to errors. When they are engaged in the creative process, they experiment freely through fields of possibilities that span the spectrums of scales of opposites. They look at the positive and negative aspects of an issue as different levels of manifestations of attributes. To the creative person, slavery and liberty are on the scale of freedom, with slavery representing very little of this attribute. Thus, they take chances with thoughts and ideas that almost invariably lead to errors, which means they wander off course. When errors appear, they do not result in paralyzing stress and frustration; to the contrary, they are integrated into the creative process. Errors are articulated broadly and put into context, so that the error can become a source of innovation.

The articulation of errors is an important strategy. The root of the word *articulation* stems from *joint*, such as a joint between limbs of the body or between the parts of speech that create sentences. An articulate speaker joins sentences together in ways that make a message coherent. The joint can both connect and separate the parts—hence, the power of articulating errors. The artist shaping a statue out of clay may squeeze and pull by error, only to be taken by surprise, and become excited with the emerging creation when the random wandering off the intended course is articulated and made part of the creation. A slip of the hands of the sculptor, the brush of the painter, or the error in the scientific laboratory, when articulated, can be joined and incorporated to innovate and invent. Errors should become a strategic posture of the minding organization.

Chaos to Order to Chaos

EMBRACING UNCERTAINTY

CHAPTER

5

Chaos to Order to Chaos

EMBRACING UNCERTAINTY

The creative process proceeds from chaos to order. The first recorded act of creation appears in the Old Testament. Genesis begins with the story of creation. To paraphrase the original Hebrew version, "In the beginning, God created the Heavens and the Earth. And the Earth was in a state of chaos."

The story continues with the acts of creation with words (God said), followed by events (there was), followed by testing (God saw that it was good), and finally naming the new creation (God named). On the sixth day, God saw all He had done, and found it to be very good. God rested on the seventh day.

The chaos gave way to order, the darkness was followed by light. This is a model for human creative endeavors. We go from chaos to order. When we are in the state of chaos, our perceptions are diffused and divergent, we expand the search in many directions and raise new questions, we break pieces and inspect them, we separate parts, we look from many different plateaus (or vantage points), and see conflicting pictures that do not fit together. We are in darkness. When we are in the state of order, our perceptions are sharpened and convergent, we constrict our focus on one direction that appears to contain the answer, we look from a platform that was built on top of the different plateaus with their conflicting sights, and we see a panorama—an unobstructed view—in which all the pieces of the puzzle fit together.

Chaos can be deliberate or emergent. When it is emergent, it is unexpected and may require unanticipated action in the form of improvisation. Often, the emergent chaos is simply the result of a question that should have been asked in the beginning to avoid undoing and redoing what had been done already in progressing from chaos to order. We have then a choice between two general models: moving from deliberate chaos to emergent order or from deliberate order to emergent chaos. The models are shown in Figure 5.1.

The model of emergent chaos calls for problem-solving skills as problems emerge. The model of deliberate chaos calls for creating chaos deliberately, up front, in the beginning (as in Genesis) by raising questions that may surface later, by focusing on problem seeking; identifying potential problems before they occur so that they can be eliminated, mitigated, or solved with adequate advanced preparation. The models of chaos to order and order to chaos can be described as deliberate prob-

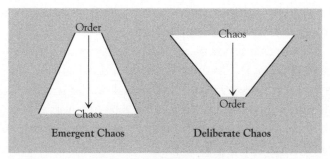

FIGURE 5.1 The difference between emergent and deliberate chaos.

lem seeking, as contrasted with emergent problem solving. If we do more of the former, there will be less need to do the latter. It also follows that the cycle time (that is, the time from the inception of an idea to its successful implementation), is shorter when we progress from deliberate chaos to order than when we proceed from an erroneous perception of order to emergent chaos. This is shown in Figure 5.2.

From Order to Emergent Chaos

Let us illustrate the model by an example. Consider the design of a new car. We follow hypothetically the stages from the inception of the idea to the release of the car to the market, first with the model of order to emergent chaos.

The design department spends a few months on conceptual designs. Once they settle on a design, they send it to engineering. The engineers may ask questions about the shape because the flow of air around the car may cause excessive drag, requiring a larger engine to maintain speed. The design may have to be undone and redone. New problems that emerge are settled and the engineering department proceeds with their own specifications and requirements. They then hand the design to manufacturing. At this stage, new questions and resulting problems emerge regarding manufacturing. These questions were not raised in the design and engineering phases. To deal

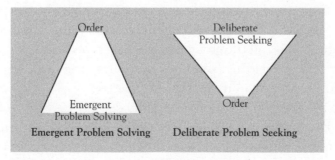

FIGURE 5.2 The difference between problem solving and problem seeking.

with the manufacturing issues, the engineering and possibly the design may have to be undone and redone. More time elapses, lengthening the cycle time. Next, suppliers of parts are brought in. Then, the assembly of a prototype takes place. The assembly may bring to light new questions leading to the emergence of new problems that require more changes. Again, work must be undone and redone. The cycle time to market continues to be delayed. Finally, the car is released to the market, with mechanics asking why it is so difficult to replace a broken washer. The answer lies partly in the fact that design was not perceived with a view for maintenance and repair.

From Deliberate Chaos to Order

Let us now follow hypothetically the stages from the inception of the idea to the release to market for the same idea using the model of deliberate chaos to order. Representatives from design, engineering, manufacturing, assembly, finance, marketing, sales, suppliers, users, and any others that may be involved at some future time, such as maintenance and repair, are all brought together in the beginning to meet in one group. The leader of the group outlines the general and possibly somewhat vague ideas. Questions may be raised for clarification and possible future elaboration. Next, the design group takes a few days to conceive a number of configurations, considering issues raised in the first meeting. A second meeting is called before the design department makes its choice, so that the designers are receptive to changes and open to input. While the designers are at work, all the group members are mobilized to look for ideas and possibilities, see problems before they emerge, and explore new ways in their areas of expertise.

Most creativity and innovation, the driving forces of productivity, lie in the minds of those closest to the work. When the alternative designs are presented to the group, issues in engineering, manufacturing, assembly, maintenance, repair, safety, customer perception of safety, comfort, and so on should all be raised. The discussion should focus on sharing perceptions. All is open and in a state of flux. If a member of the group thinks of something new or different when not in the meeting, it should be brought to the attention of the other members. As time goes on, the group coalesces and becomes a team bound by a common goal, and what is most important, more and more shared perceptions. Each team member has a heightened perception of what he or she must do in the light of sharing (not filtering and blocking) the perceptions of the other team members. Problems are found and addressed more quickly than in the linear model of order to chaos, in which the activities are performed in sequence rather than in parallel, or concurrently. There is more chaos here, more experimentation and change occur at the beginning, fewer problems need to be solved, and fewer changes need to be introduced at the end when the cost in time, money, ego, and reputation (and in customers) is high. The effect of more changes and resulting chaos in the beginning, on cycle time and quality, are shown in Figures 5.3 and 5.4.

In Figure 5.3, the thick curve shows that more effort expended early, on problem finding, results in less effort required for problem solving later on. This is the model of deliberate

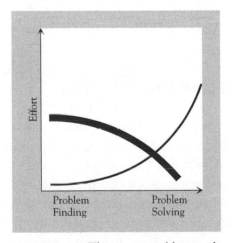

FIGURE 5.3 The more problem seeking at the beginning, the less problem solving at the end.

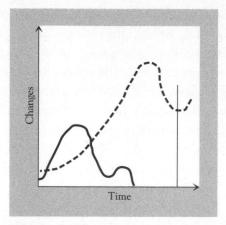

FIGURE 5.4 The more changes at the beginning, the fewer at the end.

chaos to emergent order. The thin curve shows the result of a narrow focus on order early on and emergent chaos at the end. In this case, little effort is expended in the beginning on problem finding, resulting in a heavy burden of problem-solving effort at the end.

Figure 5.4 shows that when changes are made early on, the cycle time to completion of a project is shorter. Costs of change become higher later in the project. Therefore, the solid curve representing the model of chaos to order is far superior to the dashed curve representing the model of order to chaos.

The Model of Concurrent Perception

The model of deliberate chaos to order calls for concurrent perceptions shared at the beginning, before decisions are settled in the specialized areas that act as filters. The model of concurrent perception moves us from questions to answers, from divergent perceptions to convergent perceptions, from individual creativity to team implementation, from abstract thinking to concrete action, from quick experimentation to quality results, from deliberate chaos to emergent order.

In the minding organization, chaos should deliberately be created up front. Questions need to be raised from the outset. When you start out with divergent questions, you will end up with convergent answers. When you start out with chaos, you will end up with order. This is far preferable to the scenario in which everyone coasts through a seemingly structured and orderly project and the end result is chaos.

What does it mean to encourage chaos up front? It means that everyone involved in a project should participate early. Projects take time; normally, there is a sequence of events and certain individuals are brought in at the very end. These are precisely the people you want involved from the very beginning. The design of a piece of equipment can be brilliant from an engineering, cost, aesthetic, and even marketing perspective. If, however, the person responsible for maintenance is only brought in after a prototype has been unveiled, you may be in for the rude shock that labor time for maintenance of this particular design will bankrupt you! This chaos at the end could have been prevented had the maintenance division been involved up front, in the planning and thinking stage. Chaos at the end means extensive problem solving—namely, how to make the best out of this now undesirable design. The emphasis should be on early input rather than delayed feedback.

The model of concurrent perception, in which everyone is involved early, and input is varied, multiple, and chaotic, does not mean that everyone gets their way. In the minding organization, there are not multiple minds (this would be schizophrenia); rather, the group reaches some consensus. People are uncomfortable with ambiguity and chaos, and they tend to want to make yes/no decisions as quickly as possible. Let us offer a third possibility: *yo*. Yo means neither yes nor no, and carries none of the baggage of *maybe*, which sounds more like no than yes, and which also carries the message that "I will decide the value of your idea." Yo only means "I have heard you," and "Let's see how that fits in as we move along."

Under what circumstances should you use yo? Use it whenever you are discussing anything that involves value judgment, even in the case when the decision involves you alone, and you are simply getting input from other people. In the more usual business arena, in which more than one person is involved in decision making, the use of yo should predominate.

In decision making, we put too much emphasis on the decision at the expense of the making. We jump to premature judgments, eliminating possibilities and ideas that do not immediately appear worthy of our thoughts. As action-oriented people, we do not like to spend too much time on weighing, discussing, and especially oscillating among alternatives; this aspect of the decision process is neither rewarded nor encouraged. We admire people who are quick, determined, and most of all, who get results. This, however, is not the mind-set of innovation. This is the short-term mind-set of putting out fires, not the long-term mind-set of "setting the world on fire!" with new ideas.

In the process of involving everyone early in the thinking and planning, an important consideration is to put plans into action, to try them out, without waiting for perfection. The thinking should be "good enough," not "perfect." The only way to achieve perfection is to start out with something less than perfect. Many things do not need to be perfect to work; good enough may be just that—good enough. Perfection for the secondary aspects of the business may give diminishing returns; wanting perfection for the sake of perfection may be an illness you will have to overcome. However, for the important aspects of your operation, you will have to set your sights on relentless improvement.

Relentless Improvement

The model of deliberate chaos to order is a single link, or time cycle, in a chain that keeps us moving from order to new chaos by choice, not by default or neglect. Going from chaos to order and from order to chaos, and then from chaos to order all over again, as a way of life, is a commitment to relentless improvement. It is a commitment to lifelong learning. The model of relentless improvement, shown in Figure 5.5, represents a balance between chaos and order. We do not persist in either mode too long. We begin with deliberate chaos and move to reasonable order in the form of reasonable answers to our questions; however, we never close the door to new questions and potential improvement to the answers we already have. That is why the inclined lines in the figure do not converge and meet at a point at the end of each cycle from chaos to order. The gap between the lines at the state of reasonable order is symbolic; it signifies that there is always room for improvement. As individuals, when we reach a certain stage of knowledge at the end

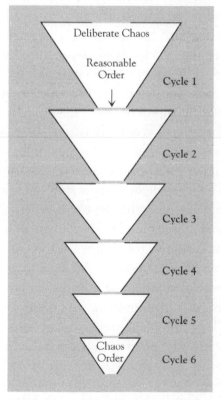

FIGURE 5.5 The model of relentless improvement.

of a learning cycle, such as the first course in a field, we move to the next cycle by taking the next course. Each cycle can be viewed as a course. When we develop a product in the first cycle time, subsequent cycles represent new, improved models of the product. The people involved in product development should assemble group members to share new perceptions in light of the experience with the first cycle from chaos to order. The group may identify new technologies that matured during the first cycle that can be used in the next generation of the product. New members may be added. For example, if purchasing from outside vendors became necessary at some point in the middle of the first cycle, it is prudent to get early involvement of a representative from purchasing and, thus, avoid time delays from undoing and redoing things that were experienced in the first cycle. In short, at the end of each cycle, we should stop to assess what we have learned so we can improve in the next cycle (see Figure 5.5).

As successive time cycles from chaos to order benefit from lessons learned, cycle times may become shorter, and this may continue with new learning in each successive cycle. When we reach a point of little improvement, it may be time to move in an entirely new direction to avoid stagnation. We may also become arrogant with our knowledge and create a filter that rejects all that does not fit our paradigm. When the paradigm becomes too rigid, it is time for a paradigm shift—a shift out of order and into chaos so we can rise to higher levels of order. Our paradigms should be viewed as unifiers of past experience, but not as rigid boundaries that limit new possibilities, including the possibility of new models and new boundaries. All paradigms should be tentative when we are committed to relentless improvement.

When Michelangelo completed his famous statue of Moses holding the Ten Commandments as he came down from Mount Sinai, he was asked how he would have made the statue if he had to do it over again. He answered in one word: "Better." There is always room for improvement. It is alleged that Michelangelo learned of an error he had made in his interpretation of the Hebrew in the Bible in which the scene of Moses descending from Mount Sinai is described. The Hebrew word *Karan* means *was shining* or *reflecting rays of light*. It could also mean *horned*, but not in the context of this story in the Old Testament. The Old Testament says that the face of Moses was radiating light, it was shining, not that he had horns. However, Michelangelo sculpted horns on the forehead of Moses. Michelangelo viewed his creation as a culmination of many cycles of target practice, with the target becoming more of a challenge with every creation, so he could continue to rise to higher levels of excellence by a commitment to relentless improvements.

To be committed to relentless improvement means to be willing to look at things in new ways, to proceed with quick experimentation, and to take risks with new ideas. This requires an environment in which errors committed in the state of chaos are not only tolerated but encouraged. This is an environment in which ongoing target practice in the state of deliberate chaos is a way of life. We discussed attitude to error earlier, but let us emphasize again that there is no learning without practice, without trial and error. It is important to realize, however, that errors are easier to fix and less costly in time, money, and frustration the earlier they occur in the cycles from the inception of the idea to its implementation. They cost the least at the stage of looking and seeing, more at the thinking and planning stages, and the most at the acting stage. Namely, the cost of error increases as we progress from chaos to order, and is very high at the final stage of perceived order. This is shown schematically in Figure 5.6, in which we plot cost of error versus stage in learning cycle.

From Order to Chaos by Default

The model of relentless improvement tries to avoid a transition from deliberate order to emergent chaos. Such transition can take place through neglect or failure to take action, by default. To safeguard against such neglect we should, whenever possi-

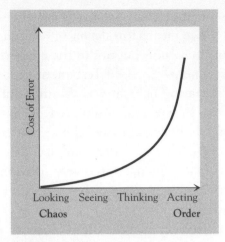

FIGURE 5.6 Cost of error versus stage in learning cycle.

ble, compare alternative courses of action and ask which are more likely to move us from order to chaos and which will preserve the order we have. Let us illustrate this with an example.

Suppose we are in the business of sorting objects. We specialize in reducing chaos to meet customer needs. A customer has received a total of 12,000 six-by-six-inch panels from two different suppliers. Each supplier shipped 6,000 panels, 1,000 of each kind. The different kinds of panels are distinguished by the figures drawn on them. Figures 5.7 and 5.8 show the six different kinds of panels made by Supplier 1 and Supplier 2. When the panels arrived in the customer's warehouse, the panels from Supplier 1 were mixed up with those from Supplier 2. The customer needs to separate the panels of the two suppliers and place them in separate cardboard boxes, 100 panels in each box. These are essentially the customer's specifications.

To identify features that will permit us to distinguish the panels of the two suppliers and separate them, we can focus on the panel figures and note the following distinguishing features for Suppliers 1 and 2:

Supplier 1's figures are simple, geometric, have a name, are made with the aid of tools such as a ruler and a compass,

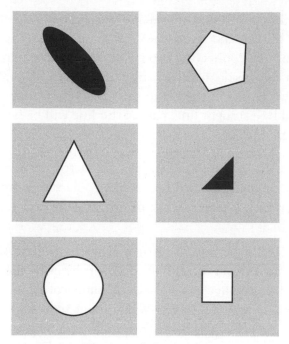

FIGURE 5.7 Panels made by supplier 1.

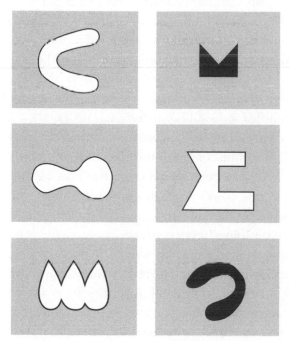

FIGURE 5.8 Panels made by supplier 2.

look like cookies that are thick in the center and not easy to break in two, and are convex. (A figure is convex when a straight line connecting two points in the figure will always be entirely inside the figure. In a nonconvex figure, you can find two points in the figure such that when they are connected by a straight line, part of the line will be outside the figure).

Supplier 2's figures are complex, not geometric, have no simple name, are made freehand, look like cookies that are thin in the center and easy to break in two, and are nonconvex.

Now comes the task of sorting. If we do not consider the consequences of our actions, we may sort by using the features described for the figures to place the panels of Supplier 1 and Supplier 2 in separate boxes. What about reducing emergent chaos? If we place a panel with a square on it in a box with panels that have circles and triangles (all Supplier 1 panels) we have the square confounded with other figures. Let us preserve order. Why not place all squares in cardboard boxes marked with squares, circles in boxes marked with circles, and so on? It is easy to proceed from this order to mixing the shapes later, but it is much more time consuming to work the other way.

Although the customer's specifications did not include the requirement for separate boxes for each figure, we should consider this possibility, ask the customer, and do more than is expected. We think of the future to guide our actions in the present. We try to perceive through the eyes of the customer to see how best to act to anticipate needs the customer may have failed to communicate to us. Relentless commitment to improving customer service means more than satisfying customer expectations or explicit wishes. It means providing even the unexpected and unanticipated to exceed customer expectations. To be able to do this calls for innovation and creativity.

Besides considering future states, concurrent perception also requires that we investigate how we got to the present situation. Why did all the panels get mixed up in the warehouse?

We could get information from the suppliers and design a process whereby the panels would be placed in the properly labeled boxes at the source and shipped directly to the customer.

Try to identify features for sorting the panels of Supplier 3 versus Supplier 4, and the panels of Supplier 5 versus Supplier 6, as shown in Figures 5.9 through 5.12.

Supplier, Processor, and Customer (SPC)

A practical application of the concurrent perception model deals with how we process work. Often, what we do is for a customer, or one who needs the results of our work. We also have suppliers, people who help us do our work. We are the customers to our suppliers. We bear the same relationship to the supplier as our customer bears to us. Namely, our customers perceive us as suppliers and they may have their own cus-

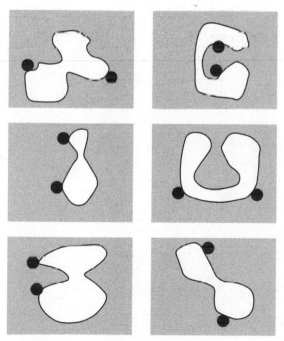

FIGURE 5.9 Panels made by supplier 3.

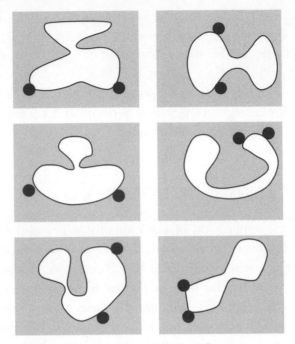

FIGURE 5.10 Panels made by supplier 4.

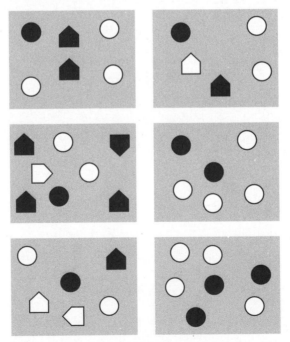

FIGURE 5.11 Panels made by supplier 5.

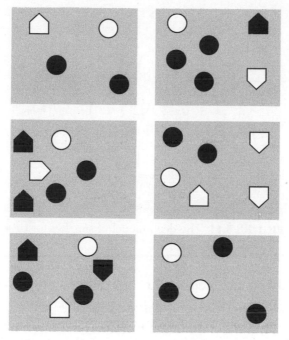

FIGURE 5.12 Panels made by supplier 6.

tomers. This chain can continue so that each can be seen as a supplier, processor, and customer. The processor is the bridge between the supplier and the customer.

To heighten our perception, we should view ourselves in all three categories, as a customer (C), as a processor (P), and as a supplier (S). In each case, we are a link in a chain. In Figure 5.13, the broken-line boundary shows how we can view ourselves as customers at the end of the top chain from S to P to C. In the middle of the figure we are in the center (P), so the processor on the top chain becomes our supplier in the middle chain, and we have a customer to our right in the middle chain. On the bottom chain of the figure, we are the supplier to a processor who has his or her own customer. Therefore, our customer from the middle chain of the figure has now become our processor on the bottom chain.

We can improve our perception of how our work is impacted by looking backward to our supplier and to our supplier's sup-

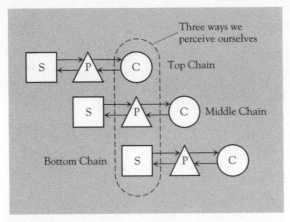

FIGURE 5.13 The deep model of supplier, processor, and customer (SPC).

plier, and by looking forward to our customer and to our customer's customer, and learning of the impact of the work we process. The deep model of supplier, processor, and customer considers chains of suppliers and chains of customers. Looking at a five-stage limit, we would consider the following elements:

Supplier's Supplier	Supplier	Processor	Customer	Customer's Customer
1	2	3	4	5

Of course, the model can be extended deeper by moving further backward, or forward, or both. Knowing how your customer will use your work may give you ideas on how to better serve customer needs; likewise, by communicating with suppliers, you may simplify and improve your process and thus pass on further improvements to the customer. Many product and service improvements originated with customers and suppliers who sparked the ideas that led to the innovations. The SPC model can also help us do more than meet customer needs and explicitly expressed desires; it may lead us to exceed customer expectations by anticipating their needs and sparking ideas for innovation.

The ability to innovate can be found at the level at which the work must be done and in the people who need and want to do the work. The innovation can originate with the processor. For example, when people at IBM wanted to move the production of printers for the personal computer to the United States instead of buying them in Japan, they encountered a problem. The printers had too many screws and other parts to make it attractive to manufacture them in the U.S. There was a need to reduce the number of parts. The engineers redesigned the printer, eliminated all the screws, and cut the total number of parts by more than one-half, thereby reducing the cost of manufacturing in the process.

In his book, *The Sources of Innovation*, Eric von Hippel documents many cases in which innovation originated with a product user, a customer, who needed a feature that was not present in the product and came up with an improvisation that the product manufacturer then adopted. Von Hippel cites in his study that customers originated 77 percent of the innovation in scientific instruments, and 90 percent in some types of plastic-forming machinery.

In some cases, innovations originate with the supplier and then are adopted by the manufacturer. For example, Edwin L. Artzt, CEO of Procter & Gamble, relates a story of how the company got an idea for an innovative solution to a problem with their Pampers disposable diapers. Procter & Gamble was having difficulty mass-producing the thin rubber used to keep the Pampers from leaking. The rubber was so thin that it would slip and fold, making high-speed production of the Pampers virtually impossible. In desperation, Procter & Gamble invited its rubber supplier to look at the creeping rubber, and an innovative solution was found. It turned out that the supplier was a leading manufacturer of ultrathin, tightly wound rubber filaments that form the cords of golf balls. A hidden, unknown similarity between golf balls and disposable diapers surfaced when the supplier and customer shared the problem. This led to a quick solution to the production problem with minimum expense.

Thus, as processors, we can innovate by learning from the customer and the supplier. The deep model of supplier, processor, and customer enhances the potential of this kind of learning and the possible resulting innovations.

Ongoing Renewal—The IWRAM Learning Model

The ongoing transitions from chaos to order are characteristic of a viable, learning, minding organization. We use the acronym IWRAM to describe the model for learning within an organization. *I* stands for individual inputs, based on insight, intuition, and information, with differing values and frameworks, coming together to create work (W). We work to reconcile different perceptions and create shared perceptions. Together we work (W), put our resolve (R) toward a common purpose (reframing and representing our mission), creating alignment (A) within the organization, and taking actions to meet our goal. Along the way, we are ever mindful to articulate errors, all the while putting our minds to work by monitoring (M) the process, modifying it as needed. The model is cyclic in that monitoring leads to new insights and information (*I*), which in turn must be worked through (W), resolve (R) must be established to align for new action (A), and monitoring (M) continues. This ongoing process is shown in Figure 5.14.

The IWRAM model shown in Figure 5.15 represents the early stages of an integrated multidisciplinary team working on a project, product, or service. Creative tensions and chaos

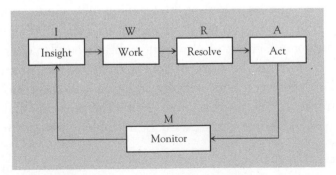

FIGURE 5.14 The cycle of ongoing renewal.

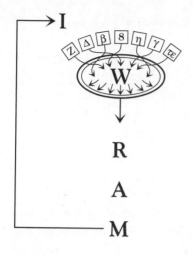

FIGURE 5.15 Early stage of team-work—chaos. From insights (*I*) to working on a shared perception (*W*), to resolve for a common purpose (*R*), to alignment for action (*A*), to minding (*M*). From this stage, order emerges.

derived from individual perceptions and agendas are represented by the misaligned squares and the shower of ideas that feed into the crucible (*W*). It is in *W* that we work through the differences in perceptions and orientations. Ideas are generated from the different perceptions and orientations that fuel innovation.

Figure 5.16 represents a mature stage of teamwork. The order, the complete alignment of team members, shown symbolically by the parallel individual squares, does not stimulate creative tension. It suggests that team members can read each other's minds.

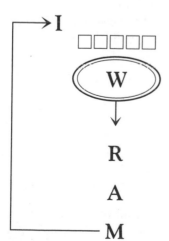

FIGURE 5.16 Mature stage of team-work—order. Differences in insights (*I*) have been worked out (*W*), the team has resolved for a common purpose (*R*), and both alignment for action (*A*) and minding (*M*) have been achieved. The sterility of order, however, must be disturbed again to spark additional creativity.

COMMITMENT AND COMPLIANCE

Figure 5.15 is the state of chaos. Figure 5.16 is the state of order. Relentless improvement calls for a reshuffling of team membership in Figure 5.16, to create a new team with the dynamics of Figure 5.15, which will eventually achieve the order of Figure 5.16, and so on, to maintain the viability of the learning and innovation cycle of ongoing renewal.

The learning and innovation cycle of ongoing renewal is based on dedicated behavior in which individuals commit to comply with reasonable team goals. In the minding organization, a member must commit to comply with the requisite steps and work involved, even if the chosen solution does not emanate from his or her individual perceptual framework. Each member must be open to the perceptual frameworks of others, and commit to comply with the path chosen by the team as a whole.

To comply in this sense means to choose to comply, in contrast with being forced to behave in some way against one's will. To achieve this type of compliance requires that everyone on the team must be open to the perceptual frameworks of other people in the organization, must be willing to converse and be open to change, and must feel that their own frame of mind and ideas are given just consideration.

When an individual feels that others have truly listened, that all frameworks have been considered with equal respect, it will be much easier to get everyone who is involved committed to the ultimate decision, even if the idea was brought on by someone else, and even if the perceptual framework is not shared by all members. The human psyche is able to commit and comply without being in complete agreement, if the mind can bridge the dissonance that results from such behavior. The key is to create a balance between commitment and compliance.

EXAMPLE

Consider a company that is a supplier of a subsystem used in an expensive machine in manufacturing operations. The subsystem consists of a spherically shaped device made up of two hemi-spheres connected by nine bolts and nuts along two flanges.

One day a young engineer came up with an idea. He had seen a new machine that could weld the two flanges of the hemispheres instead of using the bolts and nuts. Quick calcu-lation indicated a potential saving of $120 per instrument. Because the company sells thousands of these subsystems, the annual savings could be considerable.

A team representing design, manufacturing, maintenance, purchasing, marketing, sales, information systems, and human resources is convened to explore the implications of this new idea of welding the hemispheres. As is often the case, what is best from one frame of reference may be worse from another frame. The representative of maintenance, upon hearing the idea, raises a serious question. How will they replace a small part inside the sphere every three months? This required replacement of the part was the motivation for using bolts and nuts to begin with, when the subsystem was first marketed three years earlier. Institutional memory has ways of fading quickly, and the team is now discussing the past events that led to the design of the subsystem. No one has said no so far, and no resolution or conclusion has been reached; only the chaos of yo is entertained for now (somewhere between the yes of acceptance and the no of rejection).

At some point in the conversation, the representative of purchasing asks to have more details about the crucial part inside the sphere that must be replaced every three months. It turns out that the part has a short life in the environment in which it must operate, and the replacement every three months ensures that the customer will not suffer down time on a very expensive machine.

The representative of purchasing, upon hearing the detailed description of the part, jumps with excitement. A European com-pany has just announced a new line of products. One of them is a new model of the part they have been discussing. The new model is guaranteed to need no replacement for the life of the subsys-tem. The cost of the new model is $70 more than the old one.

Now, not only can the flanges be welded at a savings of $120 – $70 = $50 per subsystem, but the company saves on the cost of maintenance as well. How is the representative from maintenance feeling? The maintenance department will have 20 people who will not need to pay service calls every three months to hundreds of locations. The representative of maintenance is not saying no to the idea. In an organization committed to creativity and innovation, employees strive to make their present jobs obsolete and go on to new assignments that require new opportunities to move from chaos to order. That is why a representative from human resources was present on the team. An industrial sabbatical of two to three months can now be used to permit people from maintenance to learn new skills and acquire new tools for new products and services generated in other parts of the organization.

The minding organization creates chaos deliberately up front by starting with divergent concurrent perceptions and encourages errors to surface early when the costs of detection and correction are minimal.

Expanding the Imagination

FRAMES AS FILTERS

Expanding the Imagination

FRAMES AS FILTERS

The frames we create filter the world for us, allowing us to manage the tremendous amount of information available. When we let a single frame dominate most of our thinking, we perceive the world narrowly, losing much of the richness inherent in what we could have otherwise experienced. As the psychologist Abraham Maslow said, "When the only tool you have is a hammer, you tend to treat everything as though it were a nail." Adopting more than one frame is not easy, particularly if the primary frame you use to interpret experiences is a frame that has wide acceptance and prestige. In our society, we have a heavy bent toward a numerical framework, interpreting experiences with numbers. "Let's see the figures." "What are the statistics?" "What's the bottom line?" These are the phrases valued in conference meetings. Garrett Hardin, in his insightful book, *Filters Against Folly*, distinguishes three sig-

117

nificant filters that can be useful until, of course, they are used exclusively.

Numerical, Literate, and Ecolate Filters

The three reality macrofilters that create a manageable portfolio of the world are the numerical filter, the literate filter, and what Garrett Hardin, a prominent ecologist-philosopher, has called the ecolate filter. Briefly, numeracy focuses on quantities, proportions, and rates. Scientists and businesspeople are numerically oriented, translating reality into objects and processes that can be measured. The literate filter refers to language and an analysis of meaning through a search for the most appropriate words. The ecolate filter asks "And then what?" Time and consequences are the focus of this filter, analyzing what changes occur when a process is repeated time after time. No single filter is adequate for comprehending reality; using multiple filters gives us a more complete understanding of the world.

Too many of us rely on yet another type of filter, a specialized microfilter called an expert. Experts are people who have concentrated their filters on one particular area. Whether they have looked at the reality of which they speak through sufficiently variant filters is our responsibility to assess. Too often we are taken with jargon and verbal maneuvers, particularly if it resonates with a perspective with which we are familiar. Even more often, we are impressed by the experts armed with numbers; charts, tables, graphs, and statistics sway us to believe that every possible contingency has been considered. "The numbers speak for themselves" is a response that should make us all take notice. Numbers do not speak, and they are only models of a singular perspective on reality. Aspects of reality that cannot be easily quantified are typically left out of numerical analysis, and it is the omissions that may render inaccurate those conclusions based on the numerical filter.

Likewise, the same applies to conclusions based on verbal filters. Words are descriptions of broad categories with multiple nuances, ignoring the precision that numeracy includes. Consider the words "safe" and "unsafe," or "temporary" and "long term." Each user of these terms has a different range of experiences covered by the same word. Experts can bandy words about, encompassing a wide range of phenomena, but application to a particular process will require greater precision. We can talk about safe speeds for autos to travel, or safer work environments, but the literate filter is not enough to set policy. In another vein, how many temporary actions and processes have been in place forever? Introducing something new as temporary creates a framework for its acceptance. Again, just words, but with immense power. Hardin cautions us against the words "side effect" as having had undue influence on our thinking and on the policies we adopt as a society. "Side effect" implies that the outcome is secondary and not quite relevant enough to warrant our minding. Who is to decide which of the consequences of any action is more important? The term "side effect" effectively blocks our thinking of the total effects of a new policy, medicine, or consumer product. Surely, there are secondary or side effects, but we need to mind the process of determining those labels.

Hardin's contribution to a more balanced interpretation of reality is the ecolate filter. The ecolate filter considers the fact that we can never do merely one thing. In an organization treated as an organism, everything is connected to everything else. The ecolate filter studies this aspect of reality.

Just as context is open to interpretation, defining reality is also subjective. Which effects of your business are the primary effects, and which are secondary? It depends on your point of view. The words "it depends" are the antithesis of rigid, narrow mind-sets that view the world through single filters. When we establish something as "fact," we ignore the context in which it is a fact. Surely, this simplifies thinking, allowing us to take in multitudes of pieces of information, but to what end? When we stuff our heads with facts, uprooting them from the contexts in which they may have degrees of truth, we are engaged in single-faceted thinking. Unfortunately, education consists mainly of this type of mental activity. Only in our later years, after thinking styles have been ingrained, do we suddenly learn that, actually, it depends. Theories, hypotheses, models, and probabilities are far less stable than the "facts," which we have accepted as givens. When children are taught facts, they come to view the world as rigid and stable, and these are the thinking styles that ensue. Teaching children early about the concepts of hypotheses and probabilities creates a frame of mind conducive to creativity and innovation, to serve a lifetime.

The two primary filters we rely on to interpret experience, namely the numerical and literate, penetrate our minds from the early stages of our education, ingraining these two modes of information manipulation. Our mental abilities are judged on the basis of our use of these filters, and IQ tests have traditionally tested our mathematical-logical thinking and our linguistic abilities. Howard Gardner, a Harvard psychologist, has set forth a more encompassing view of intelligence, rejecting the notion that thinking is composed of these two factors alone. Gardner argues against the two filters as the sum of our ability to comprehend the world. He has identified seven types of intelligence that we each possess to some degree, two of which are the filters we have already discussed, the numerical and literate. The other less conventional intelligences are spatial (seen in engineers and pilots), bodily kinesthetic (dancers, surgeons), musical (composers), interpersonal (understanding others, as psychologists), and intrapersonal (understanding one's own self, as poets). These intelligences are the equivalent of filters, any one of which will give us a different perspective and interpretation of a shared experience. With each filter, an individual will creatively interpret an experience differently than someone else using the same filter. We can see, then, that the possibilities are enormous, the opportunities for innovation are abundant, but so are the chances for miscommunication, misunderstanding, and malfunction.

Balancing Resources

One of the reasons we view the world through filters and create categories into which we fit our experiences is that our cognitive capabilities are limited; there is only so much information we can process at any one time. Information itself, however, is an unlimited resource. New discoveries and creations add to our body of knowledge and information, thus increasing the information resource. There is such exponential growth in amounts of information produced, and ease in accessing copious quantities of it, that our most serious problem lies in the resource limitations of the human mind to process and integrate the wealth at hand.

We also know that outside resources are limited. Our internal filters may deceive us into a false sense of what those outer limitations really are. Many limits are set arbitrarily and then adhered to as though carved in stone. For example, once a budget is set in an organization and funds are allocated, when an unexpected need arises, it is often difficult to rearrange the budget to accommodate the change. Other limitations are determined by our frames of reference and working outside those limitations never occurs as a possibility. Many of the records people break are goals that other individuals had previously declared to be humanly impossible to attain.

Most of the limitations imposed within organizations go to unnecessary and debilitating extremes, primarily because of perceived limitations of available resources. The most common resources considered are money, time, and talent. "It will cost too much," "It will take too long," "That would require a full-time specialist," are the types of statements reflecting a belief in limited resources, reflecting limited abilities.

A limited resource we can all relate to is time. Even when money is plentiful and talent available, time is an equal opportunity resource. Each of us has the same 24 hours in a day. Our conceptions of time, however, play a large part in our use of this limited resource. What is "not enough time?" What is "short term" versus "long term?" What time frame is included when we say "in the long run?" More practically, do we focus our efforts on processes for the here and now, or do we consider the effect we may have on our great-great-great grandchildren? All of our choices are time bound, and balancing our decisions must take this measure into consideration.

The Federal Reserve Board is a good example of an organization that must constantly consider time. Changing interest rates, inflation, accruing greater national debt, and the like, may increase current popularity but lead to later dangers, or decrease current popularity for later gain. Rarely are the difficult choices winners in the short and long term (again, the numerate interpretation is critical for time). Every organization has similar issues to contend with. How much time do we give for a process to prove itself against alternatives? How much money are we willing to spend within that time frame? Every decision must be balanced on the scale of time.

Because of limited resources, organizations end up thinking in terms of "all-or-none," focusing only on the extremes. For example, if computer equipment needs to be updated, do we have to revamp the entire system? If resources are limited, computers can be updated a little at a time, in stages. Instead, organizations either complete the entire task or do nothing at all. Improvements in increments are not encouraged, going back to our obsessions with outcome rather than process. Our desires and demands need to be balanced with the resources available. Fortunately, human ingenuity and inventiveness have no given limits, and our ability to tackle issues within organizations through balanced and flexible measures is a renewable resource.

The Tragedy of the Commons

Minding the resources that are limited is a task requiring considerable thoughtfulness. If resources are valuable but finite, the question becomes "who gets them?" Garrett Hardin proposed the name "tragedy of the commons" for a principle originally laid out in 1832 by Oxford professor William Forster Lloyd. Imagine yourself a herdsman on an African desert, living peacefully with other herdsmen on shared commons. Suppose that the total herd population has just reached the carrying capacity of the land, but you have a chance to acquire 10 more animals. Should you add these animals to your herd? Because the additional animals exceed the carrying capacity of the land, all of your animals will end up with a little less food, as will the animals of the other herdsmen. Nevertheless, you expect a net gain from the added animals because any gain is all yours, whereas the loss (in available food) is shared among all the herdsmen. Your share of the gain is 100 percent, whereas your share of the loss is a small fraction of the total. Balancing your gain against your loss, the rational decision is to add the animals to your herd. Every other herdsman with access to the common resource will reach the same decision. When they all add 10 animals to their herds, famine ensues and the entire system collapses. The system in which we share the common resources ends in disaster when each person considers individual gain against communal losses. Herein lies the tragedy of the commons. The scenario, which appears to be a win-lose zero-sum game (one player wins what the other loses), ultimately degenerates into a lose-lose nonzero-sum game (both players lose) when the true dynamics of the system are played out over time.

Such decisions are not restricted to African herdsmen. Businesses share a commons in finite numbers of consumers with finite numbers of dollars to spend. Introducing another brand on the market may be akin to adding another 10 animals to the herd. Manufacturers share finite natural resources. Disposing of manufacturing wastes into landfill or creating products from raw materials uses up and takes away those same resources from others. Entertainers vie for finite audience leisure time as networks compete for finite amounts of advertising dollars. University departments compete for finite funding. Each wants to add to their herd. We must mind which of our resources can be shared widely without loss, and which must be shared through a policy of balance.

Recognizing the limits of our global commons makes the development of accounting systems of responsibility more likely. Changes that are touted as "developments" and "improvements" will have to face this accounting system instead of just drowning us in a wave of attractive verbiage. Because information and human ingenuity are resources that know no bounds and have no tragic end from common usage, we can optimistically say that the rest is manageable.

The Cyclic Process of Minding

The complicated activities we undertake produce consequences that are good, as well as consequences that are bad, consequences we can predict as well as consequences that are unexpected. Understanding these relationships forces us to look at a broader reality, and not just the segment of reality that suits us. When we consider the big picture, we get a balanced sense of causes and effects, rather than a myopic tunnel vision of just a single factor at great depth.

For example, people are killed every year in traffic accidents. According to Hardin, were we to focus on this factor alone, and declare zero tolerance for traffic deaths, then automobile transportation would be outlawed in the United States. Instead, we look at both the positive and negative consequences of automobile use, and we accept that the car, although not a perfect tool, is one we want to use. Although banning cars because they have lethal potential sounds absurd, other laws following similar logic have been passed in the United States. Food additives that have any cancer-causing potential at any level of concentration in any animal, as well as medicines that have potential negative consequences in any fraction of the population, have been restricted even if the potential benefits greatly outweigh the potential dangers. The whole concept of what is safe is typically reduced to a passionate exchange of words for whichever particular health issue is in vogue. At any given time, a certain food is declared unsafe and people drop it completely from their diets. Eggs, butter, red meat, and wax-covered apples have all been vilified, but then the nation's consciousness is diverted to the next foodstuff while being told it is now safe to have a couple of eggs a week. Everything is dangerous at some level.

Absolute reliability is contrary to the human experience. This is true both of the individual and of systems created by individuals. Life experiences are fraught with negative consequences; this is the essence of human drama. Systems designed to circumvent unreliability fail to take into account the human aspect. Insisting on a zero tolerance for negative consequences paralyzes us into inaction, which itself will have negative consequences. For example, if we demand zero contamination of our ocean swimming water, we must first ask what exactly constitutes contamination. We need a numerical consensus describing contamination. Suppose that a contaminant is deemed not harmful if present at 10 percent concentration, so to be safe, we close the beaches if the contaminant is found at 5 percent, and commence cleanup tactics. Some environmentalists may demand removal of the contaminant to 0 percent. Is this wise? The ability to reduce a contaminant from 10 to 5 percent is not the same as reducing the contaminant from 5 to 0 percent. Trying to reach the extremes or absolutes in any system has a high price, the benefits of which may not be warranted. Committing ourselves to achieve the extreme of one dimension by definition creates a debt on another dimension. Plato, the Greek philosopher, lamented 2,400 years ago in his book *The Republic:* "In the seasons, in plants, in the body, and above all in civil society, excessive action results in violent transformation into its opposite."

The process of minding is cyclic because feedback brings us back to reassess and modify our original inputs. In a cyclic system, anything that gets exaggerated or unduly deflated has an effect on everything else in the system. Some effects are more direct than others, but reverberations filter through permeable boundaries. We can create a negative effect out of any attribute by exploiting boundaries. For example, commitment is a positive principle. When present in good measure, we find dedication. Out of proportion, the result is fanaticism on the high end, and passivity on the low end. When we are balanced in decision making, we are flexible. The two negative extremes of flexibility are rigidity on one end, and vacillation on the other end.

Responsibility with Authority: Creating an Organization That Functions like the Human Body

Distributing responsibility and authority among a group instead of entrusting all to a single individual is key to becoming a minding organization. Like the art project a five-year-old brings home from school, if all the glue is in one place, pieces of the project are bound to fall apart. Spread the glue around, and the project remains intact. It may appear that persons in an organization are embued with responsibility, but in reality, if they do not have authority, the only responsibility they have is to follow the direction of the person with authority. Ultimate responsibility lies with the person who has authority, and authority is the glue.

This type of organization functions more like the human body. There are local control centers, each responsible for its function, with the authority to take charge and change, but always working within the framework of the larger system. For example, if you are suddenly face-to-face with a leopard, your flight mechanisms do not need to get approval from some central authority that must decide whether to continue pumping blood to the digestive system because you just ate lunch, or whether blood should be delegated to this new need to flee. By then, you would be lunch. The same kind of local control centers can be found in minding organizations.

The phrase "all in good measure" dictates that authority should not be "all or none." Not every function should be able to make decisions with the potential to bankrupt the entire system. The great inability of managers to give up control stems from the fear that they will have to give up complete control, in effect, giving another entity all the functions over which they have had control. The idea is to allow individuals who are supposed to carry out various functions the ability to confront dilemmas facing them in their task with tools that can resolve problems and improve the system.

Meanwhile, instead of management spending time resolving issues that can be dealt with more effectively locally, more effort can be put toward coordinating the now better-functioning sub-systems, and planning for change and growth. Peter Senge, in his book, *The Fifth Discipline*, speaks of "learning organizations" that have adopted this mode of operation. Most managers with whom he worked had little time for thinking, reflecting, and doing other cognitive big-picture work because of incessant busy-ness that drives the typical workday, keeping them from important business.

Every organization, whatever its size, can benefit from implementing a localization of responsibility and authority. Organizations as large as government bureaucracies and as small as individual families have gained when the glue is spread out. For example, the California Board of Education, a monolithically large organization, has adopted a policy that spreads the control from school districts down to the individual schools. School site councils have been established, involving teaching and support staff from a school, as well as parents and community members within the school. The principle underlying the creation of site councils is that those individuals who are most affected by the operation of the school should have a major role in the decisions regarding how their school functions. The council is responsible for developing a school improvement plan, budgeting funds in a way that is supportive of the plan, and continuously reviewing and assessing the effectiveness of the plan with periodic updates. For example, in one elementary school, bringing technology into the school was incorporated by the site council into the improvement plan, and the council had the authority to decide how to spend an allocation for this plan. Heated debate ensued over whether an additional computer should be purchased for the developing computer laboratory or whether a class would get a set of graph calculators for algebra and trigonometry students. The decision makers were those with firsthand knowledge of the school's needs, and more important, were those who would most be affected by the decision. Thus, the decision was handled with different considerations than those that would surface had it been made by a board far removed from the context of the problem.

In the same sense, a family can also be a minding organization. In a strictly hierarchical family, parents make the decisions and see themselves as the only ones with the authority to do so. Junior is not allowed to drink soda for breakfast, he is not allowed to watch television before doing homework, and parents make all the rules. Some parents create this atmosphere out of love and concern for their children, truly believing that father knows best. Others do so because they think that the only alternative is the kind of permissiveness in which the parent relinquishes control and the child takes over. In either case the outcome is the same; one side feels victimized. The reality is that there is another alternative, just as there is another alternative in business organizations. Command and control need not be relinquished for anarchy. Parent-child and management-employee relations do not have to be either win-lose or lose-win. Thomas Gordon has inspired a win-win method for families in his exciting book, *Parent Effectiveness Training*, that is equally applicable for any organization that wants to mind itself and improve. Solutions, actions, and behaviors must be acceptable to both sides. That's it. Neither side imposes their will on the other side, neither side gives in; a solution or action is not implemented until it is mutually agreed upon.

Can Junior have soda for breakfast? If the child demands it and the parent refuses, the child's role is diminished. If the parent does not want the child to drink soda but relents, then the parent's role is diminished. The parent and child are going to have to achieve a solution that satisfies both of them. In the process, they will become more familiar with each other's needs and values, and the system becomes easier to manage. For example, through a conversation, it may come out that what the child really wants is a drink with fizz. By creative problem solving, the child may suggest infusing seltzer water into a glass of orange juice. This may be the alternative that is mutually acceptable. If not, they keep thinking! The most important tenet is that those involved in the decision do not have the will of someone else imposed upon them. Both assume the responsibility to solve the issue, and both have authority to reject a proposal.

Because this sounds so great (e.g., a healthy drink satisfying the parent, fizz satisfying the child, and an elimination of the conflict and tension that otherwise would permeate the breakfast table), why do people resist changing?

Adopting a balance of responsibility and authority across the organization, be it family, private enterprise, or government agencies, is one of the most radical departures from tradition, going against tenets instilled in us since we ourselves were children. We grow up with authority figures and educate ourselves for the day when we will become someone else's authority figure. In the classroom, we learn about heroes who invariably worked alone, assuming sole responsibility and authority. Our cinematic heroes are cut from similar cloth. Only in sports do we admire team efforts, but even there, the captain has the authority to make calls and the responsibility to delegate the moves; other team members do not have this stature. We therefore do not have a mental model with examples, demonstrating the effectiveness of team players, be it sports, politics, education, or business, who share responsibility and authority.

In addition, there is no numerical method to quantify the benefits to be gained through these changes in approach. We cannot compare the various strategies and assess their effects on the bottom line. So the voice in the back of our head says,

"Better the devil you know than the devil you don't." To these critics, a review of the section on error (Chapter 4) is in order! Practicing, implementing, trying the ideas in various measures and arenas, will be the proving ground each of us will require. There is no magic formula, no single method that can be applied across the board. Minding means finding the fit that is right for the organization. The criteria of judgment need only be the satisfaction of the people involved, however it is measured. Copying the format implemented by another organization or emulating a solution that works for a so-called leading firm is not going to be effective in the way that a solution that is generated by the people involved can be. The difference between emulating a solution and generating one yourself is the difference between hearing about someone else's vacation and taking one yourself.

Kniht Backward

VISIT THE FUTURE IN THE PRESENT

Kniht Backward

VISIT THE FUTURE IN THE PRESENT

A large university completed construction, planted grass in the open spaces, but delayed plans for paved paths between buildings. The people who walked daily on campus soon left a network of visible paths on the grass. It was this network of paths that was paved. The university had no problems with people trampling grass and flower beds.

Plans and Planning

What is it exactly that constitutes a plan? At one level it is a framework that allows us to look into the future, guided by what has transpired in the past. If we limit ourselves to only that which has transpired in the past, then we never move beyond that which we have already done. Thus, a plan for the future incorporates the past as well as our perceptions of what changes will be required to succeed in the future.

The concept of plan has different meanings based on whether we consider plan as a noun or a verb. As a noun, "plan" is an inanimate object. However, as a verb, "planning" implies generating momentum and having the agility and ability to change course. Once plan becomes a noun in the minds of the group responsible for it, the thinking process ends. The plan becomes embedded in the collective mind as an immovable anchor that dictates all other movements by the group. When planning remains a verb, and maintains its status as a process through which the group is thinking about the future, it is a flexible catalyst for the group's activities.

The emphasis on "plan" as a verb, not as a noun, is crucial in the world of quick turnarounds. Planning must be an ongoing process, an integral part of thinking. A plan is based on assumptions of what the future will require. As the future unfolds, not all our assumptions will bear out and our plan will then be deficient.

The way most groups organize for planning makes the process one of carving out and delegating, evaluating current performance to create a new set of rules to set in stone. There is usually a "planning department," which takes on the burden of setting a new plan, and once the plan is finalized, it is implemented. The whole process is one of rigid steps resulting in a weighty, inflexible, and often frustrating set of rules and goals.

The notion of creating a plan is based on the assumption that the time frame for the plan's implementation is a fixed property that has no influence on the success of the plan. Creating a five-year plan assumes that the five years will unfold as assumed in the plan. In our world of increasing flux, conceptualizing time in this manner is outdated. Even a six-month plan may require modifications. Time has never stood still, but it now races around, spewing forth unanticipated sparks that we must prepare ourselves to embrace. A rigid plan forces us to look the other way, until we are literally hit over the head with change. This is no way to face the future. This is not minding.

Minding means that the reality is more important than any plan, and we set ourselves up to incorporate changes.

These are not abstractions to be put aside, but rather ideas to start using today. For example, suppose you have planned a presentation at work, and you have 20 minutes to speak. After the first 5 minutes, you realize that you will be unable to say everything you planned to say in 20 minutes. People are interested and asking questions that you did not anticipate. The reality does not mesh with your plan. What do you do? You must adjust your plan. We have all been at lectures in which the speaker says something like, "We are behind, so let's keep moving," and then proceeds to cut off a great discussion to stick with the plan. You can actually feel the energy in the room dissipate when a speaker does this. Most people would be thrilled to hear the speaker say, "I had planned to talk about other things, but this discussion is promising, so let's forget my plan." Very often, a sidetrack is a tributary that may be just as important as the original plan. Even calling it a "sidetrack" detracts from its potential importance and imposes a judgment; the main track is the serious stuff, and sidetracks keep us away and waste our time. Once again, our choice of words is a way to frame and reframe the way we think. Do not dismiss these tangents because they were not part of the plan. At times, the so-called side effects may be more important than the main effect.

Plan Backward—Kniht

Human beings are capable of delayed gratification. We work hard even when the fruits of our labor are weeks or months away. Even children can comprehend that effort expended now will result in a reward later on. (Animals are incapable of this understanding; you cannot tell a dog to roll over now because tomorrow you will give him three bones.) Our ability to understand that current activity has a bearing on future outcomes is a forceful element in planning.

Humans can thus contemplate the future, create visions of desired states, and cognitively think backward (kniht) to assess the efforts that will be required to achieve the vision. A plan to achieve the vision is an educated guess, a structured process that is one of several possible choices that will bridge the gap between the current state you are in and the desired state of your vision. You can have varying levels of confidence in various aspects of your plan, and with an open-minded approach the planning evolves. One method for evolving a plan is working backward.

Planning means creating a desired goal state and then assessing what you must start doing now to achieve the goal. The only thing you are relatively sure of is the goal you have set. A reasonable first step is to ask yourself what would be the last step you would need to take just before you reach your goal. Working backward, you then assess what the next-to-last step will have to be, and so on, until you have worked yourself all the way to the first step in the process. We frequently do this in our daily lives; we do not do this often enough for the longer-term issues. For example, if you must get to the office by 9:00, but you want to spend an hour in the gym before work, your line of thought may sound like this: "To be at work at 9:00, I have to leave the gym by 8:30; to leave the gym by 8:30, I have to be in the shower by 8:00, which means I have to get to the gym by 7:00; therefore, I must leave the house by 6:30." Working backward brings you to the hour you have to get up in the morning. Based on what you want for the future, you know what you must do now. If it were 6:45 and you still had not left the house, you might berate yourself, "I'm already late!" You are only late based on the plan you have created. Thus, our assessments of our current state are couched in our planning of the future.

What happens with long-term planning? There are so many unknowns that people prefer to deal with the here and now and deal with the future as it unfolds. People will say, "We'll cross that bridge when we come to it," and ask each other, "Where should we begin?" The trouble is that if you don't deal with the future in the present, there may be no bridge to cross when you get there!

When we look to the future for a desired goal and work backward, we are able to sustain hardships and unpleasantness in our current state because we know that there is a reason for the steps we are taking. Few people want to suffer just for the sake of suffering, but in the context of striving for a desired goal, most people will endure what they would otherwise shun. An extreme example of such vision is the suffering Nelson Mandela willingly took upon himself to realize his vision of South Africa. Years of imprisonment and separation from family would have been avoided had he only renounced his goals to end apartheid. Mandela refused the government offers of freedom in return for such a declaration. Unwavering in his commitment to the goal, inspired by the fundamental importance of his mission, his resolve inoculated him against the immense personal cost. Mandela's persistence and strong sense of purpose paved the way to liberation and triumph after 27 years in prison.

Do More with Less

When we start from the current state and work forward, we tend to look at the resources presently available to us and ask what is the best way to use them to achieve possible futures. When we work backward, we first determine the goal that is worthy of our efforts, and then get to the point of asking what resources we must currently develop to achieve our goal. When we work forward, we only work with the resources currently available; that is, we "work within our means." When we work backward, we may find ourselves stretching our resources, having to "work beyond our means," but in so doing, reaching heights that forward planning would never have attained. By working backward, we may find ourselves creating ways to do more with less, finding ways to work smarter rather than harder. Working backward is a way of forcing more of the problems to surface at the outset rather than at the end, creating chaos at the beginning for order to more likely emerge at the end.

To work smarter and to do more with less takes practice. Adding frameworks to our cognitive repertoire adds smartness; working backward is one such framework that filters out mental limitations we have placed on resources.

Force Future Problems to Surface in the Present

Many organizations embark on new product or service development by paying very superficial and limited "visits" to the future. For example, an idea for a new, more precise instrument for measuring and controlling temperature in a complex environment may excite the technical people in the organization. An assessment of cost and potential profits from sales, at a price that is based on adding a profit margin to the cost of manufacturing and sales, is rooted in a tradition of working from a present assessment of cost, over which we can exercise some control to determine a price, which is to be realized in the future, over which we have less control. The price is based on customers' perceptions of value associated with the product. If we proceed with cost first and price last, we may end up with serious problems in the future when our cost exceeds the price the customers are willing to pay for the product.

To force such potential problems to surface early, before we embark on implementing the idea for a new product (or service), it is very powerful to begin with price and work backward to cost.

From Price to Cost

Imagine a company that designs instruments for industrial use and that is committed to innovation as a way of life. Every year more than one-half of their sales in dollars are generated from sales of instruments that did not exist in the market three years earlier. Here is how this company achieves this high level of innovation, working backward from price to cost.

PHASE 1: LIVE IN THE WORLD OF THE CUSTOMER

Each year teams of people representing various departments, such as engineering, manufacturing, and marketing, arrange visits to a key customer (both existing and potential) for a few days to study customer needs.

Suppose that one of the teams became aware of a problem in a customer's plants. The vice president in charge of manufacturing revealed that they operate in a very tough environment in which it is difficult to measure and control temperature. As a result, cost of energy is very high. When they were small and had only one plant and were in the unique position of being the originators of a new product, they paid little attention to cost containment. Now with 127 plants all over the world and competition coming into the market, they are under pressure to cut prices, and therefore they are looking at ways to reduce costs of manufacturing.

The engineer on the visiting team inquires about the temperature control device and the instruments employed in the system. After a few calculations on the back of an envelope, he asks the vice president what difference it would make if they could lower the temperature fluctuations from the present high range of 10 degrees to less than 1 degree. The VP responds with excitement: "What difference? We would pay any price to have such a control capability. Do you know how much we could save in energy? And that is not all. The quality of the special ceramic tiles we produce would be enhanced, and our yield would increase. This would be a provocative innovation. Our engineers have tried to achieve lower fluctuations in temperature, but the range of 10 degrees is as low as they could get it."

The team has unearthed a customer need, in 127 plants for this customer alone; however, the value perceived by the customer is still a mystery. "We would pay any price" cannot be taken literally. It is now time to assess what the energy savings will be in each plant. How much will yield increase? Will it be 98 percent instead of 90 percent? What is the associated cost saving? Further exploration leads to an assessment that the cost savings for a plant could be on the order of $10,000 per month. Now the team may have a reasonable idea of the price for a new control system that limits temperature fluctuations to one degree. However, we are not done yet.

PHASE 2: BRING THE FUTURE BACK HOME

Upon returning to their company, the teams share their findings from visits to the customers, where they lived in the customers' world for a week. It turns out that another team observed that a customer they visited had a similar problem of temperature control. However, this customer manufactures a state-of-the-art product, and their savings per month could reach $100,000, but they need to limit fluctuations in temperature to less than one-tenth of a degree. The customer even indicated that they would be willing to participate in the cost of developing such a system and would agree on a price schedule up front. This manufacturer has three plants.

We can now assess a reasonable price based on customers' needs and their perception of value. We are also aware of two different markets: one consists of about 12,000 plants (127 for the customer we visited, who is the largest, and the rest are other manufacturers); the other consists of only three plants. We have the following alternatives:

Alternative 1: Choose the market with the large volume.

Alternative 2: Choose the market with the small volume.

Alternative 3: Choose both markets.

Alternative 4: Choose neither market.

PHASE 3: WORKING BACKWARD FROM PRICE AND VOLUME TO COST

Now teams can assess the cost of developing systems for Alternatives 1 and 2. The volume can be used to calculate savings resulting from economy of scale when purchasing parts from suppliers. Once costs are established, the teams compare them with price and decide which of the four alternatives is most viable in terms of the ratio of value created over resources required.

Shorten Cycle Time

To build a communication satellite used to take about nine years. Thinking backward resulted in reducing the cycle time from conceptualization to launch from nine years to seven to five to three, then to 18 months, and now to weeks, to the point that there are now plans for a satellite factory. Thinking backward helped identify future problems early in terms of the need for precision assemblers and their training, need for financial resources, need to form alliances with other manufacturers, and so forth. The process set the stage for changing the way things were done in the past and learning to leverage limited resources to do more with less.

Get What You Want

In 1970, my wife and I decided to move to a home that would be within walking distance from UCLA. The brokers showed us homes they believed we could afford. None were within walking distance from UCLA. After one year of search we gave up.

We then approached the search backward. Instead of beginning with the present, namely our resources at the time, and exploring houses on the market compatible with the resources, we turned the process around. We decided to visit the future.

We went to a house that both my wife and I liked very much and that was within walking distance from UCLA. We rang the doorbell even though the house was not on the market. It did not work out, but the people, Dr. Morris Beckwitt and his wife Ellen, became very close friends. This shows you the side benefits you can reap by venturing off the beaten paths of traditional thinking, planning, and working.

We did not give up and we rang the doorbell of another house. This house was also not on the market, but we wanted it as our future home. Six months later we moved into the house. It was not an easy process; we knew what we wanted, but when we discovered the owner's price, we had a problem. We created ways of doing more with less, but with an eye to the future it was well worth the effort.

Bring the Future to the Present

When we employ the process of concurrent perception (discussed in Chapter 5), we bring future perceptions and knowledge to the present. For example, in bringing the construction inspector to the building site from the very beginning, we have the future perceptions of inspection available and in action in the present. Likewise, having the perceptions of the assembly line worker early, in the present, allows us to see the problems they would otherwise see in the future. The process of concurrent perceptions brings the future to the present.

You can attempt to visit your future house as well as your future profession. Think of the many people who spend years studying and preparing for a profession that they end up disliking. Resources of time, money, energy, and human vitality could be conserved if we had a program for young people to visit in the present the professions of the future. Each summer a 16-, 17-, or 18-year-old could be assigned to a mentor—an engineer, nurse, doctor, teacher, lawyer, accountant, or any professional in a line of work of interest to them. They would shadow the mentor for a few weeks, and in so doing, would get a glimpse of the future.

The teen would bring what they perceived as their future to the present. The results of the experience would either reinforce the pursuit of the profession and generate a strong commitment, or it might lead to a desire to visit other futures.

Producers of products, service providers, suppliers, and customers would all remove much of the uncertainty and chaos of the future if they would make it a habit to devise creative ways to visit the future and bring the future to the present. Visit the company that has in the present the very attributes you wish to possess in the future. Live in that world for awhile, and in so doing, you will experience the future in the present. This does not necessarily mean visiting companies in your own industry. The process may at times benefit from a creative notion, such as visiting a fire department to see how your company might deliver a service with the same sense of urgency in an unpredictable market as firefighters do.

The Containers Problem

Try to employ the process of thinking backward to solve the following problem. You are given two asymmetrical, oddly shaped, translucent containers with a capacity for nine and four ounces, respectively. You also have a large vat of brown liquid. When you put the liquid in the containers, the level can be seen through the translucent containers, but the containers are not marked to indicate a quantity. How would you proceed to measure exactly six ounces of the liquid, using only these two containers?

We are taught how to think forward. However, in this problem you know where you want to end—with six ounces in the larger container. You do not know where to begin. Try to think backward to find a solution. For that matter, how would you measure four and one-half ounces? Or, one and one-third ounces?

In the minding organization, thinking backward allows you to literally bring emerging knowledge and perceptions of the future to the present.

The New Leadership

OPERATING ON THE EDGE OF CHAOS

The New Leadership

OPERATING ON THE
EDGE OF CHAOS

To create an adaptive, innovative, problem-solving organization requires a new form of leadership, the ability to provide guidance in the search for purpose and goals. Classical leadership—implementing stipulated goals—is committed to the status quo. The new leadership requires courage to question the known present. This is more daring than investigating the unknown future. The new leadership is constantly challenging norms. The classical leadership can lead in a state of order, but it loses control in chaos and conflict. The new leadership thrives on leading in chaos and conflict.

Technical problem solving encompasses skills that provide answers to posed questions. Adaptive, creative problem solving begins with a search for questions for which there are no known skills to provide answers. It is also focused on detecting inappropriate questions. To spot a wrong question may require more creativity than to spot the wrong answer.

The environment in which the new leadership emerges is one of adaptive creativity in which people lead with and without authority. The person at the top of the organization in the role of classical leadership is known as a chief executive officer, or CEO. The new CEO must learn to operate on the edge of chaos, and become an OEC. The new leader creates an environment of distributed decision making and distributed leadership throughout the organization. Leadership is exercised by all, where and when it's needed, as judged by people working and adapting to the future as it unfolds.

The role of leadership in this new age is to create the environment that can free the mind to tap the powers of the human brain. This role calls for the ability to provide people with a global perspective and a sense of purpose of the organization, so as to give meaning to their efforts to achieve goal states at the local level in their day-to-day work.

The challenge to new leadership is to develop in people an adaptive capacity to work creatively in a rapidly and constantly changing environment. This demands that leaders counteract people's tendencies to become dependent and passive, and instead, to call for their creative adaptation to change and their exercise of leadership and initiative without waiting for explicit authority to do so.

Such is an environment for ongoing learning, in which people learn to adapt through action-based creativity, with top leadership carrying the burden while learning is in progress.

Leadership in the Minding Organization

Thomas Jefferson wrote, "I know of no safe repository of the ultimate powers of society but the people themselves; and if we think them not enlightened enough to exercise their control with a wholesome discretion, the remedy is not to take it from them, but to inform their discretion."

Leaders in the new model for the minding organization will infuse people with ongoing learning to inform their discretion. They will focus on context more than on content. They will articulate a sense of purpose and let the people surprise them with their capacity for creativity, innovation, and self-organization to adapt to the chaos and uncertainty of an unpredictable future. These leaders will assume the role of conductors, to orchestrate early involvement of all those involved in the life cycle of a project—employees, suppliers, and customers—to achieve concurrent perception. They will say yo (yes and no), rather than no, to new ideas and thus permit quick experimentation.

Leaders in the minding organization will give people the authority to solve problems locally. At each level of work, people will be given the responsibility to be right and the authority to be wrong. Leaders will show respect for people and respect for their ideas, when right or wrong. Excellence will be rewarded in all the forms in which it can be manifested in the life and work of the minding organization.

At the global level, leaders will begin a project with a frame that is rich in possibilities, chaotic as this may be early on, by starting with statements of purpose that can expand imaginations. Once a sense of grand purpose is adopted, it will become an attractor. All efforts at the local level throughout the organization will become trajectories that follow tributaries that drain into the attractor.

Creating a Sense of Purpose

In our backyard we have a lemon tree that, for years, bore huge fruits year-round. One year the tree suddenly stopped bearing fruits. No amount or type of fertilizer helped restore the tree to its former viable state. After two years, the gardener suggested that the tree was probably old and would soon die. There were in fact many dry branches and signs of deterioration. Then one day my nephew, Uri, an agricultural engineer, came for a visit.

When I showed him the tree, he reached for a green branch and snapped it, almost breaking it off. As the branch hung limply, I yelled that he was breaking the tree. He replied that what he was doing was reviving the tree, helping it rejuvenate, giving it purpose. With his guidance, I adapted and joined him, leaving half of the tree with broken branches. Within a few weeks the tree came to life! It has been four years now and the tree is thriving. I have since used the method on other trees with remarkable success.

Purpose is central. Think of the broken branches; think of Nelson Mandela in prison; think of Holocaust victims struggling to survive in the concentration camps. Viktor Frankl, who survived the Holocaust, attributed his survival to the will to create meaning in his book, *Will to Meaning*. When people know and share in a desire to achieve the purpose of the organization, what they do has meaning. They know the why and what for, and can persist sometimes against all odds. Watch a baby, contemplate the complexity of its system, and marvel at the capacity for self-organization as the child thrives on the edge of chaos. The baby learns to crawl, then seemingly spontaneously, to walk, then talk. The attractor that drives the process of adapting is the innate and compelling force of purpose: the will to survive. Later on in life this purpose gets recharged with additional purposes, the most profound being the will to create meaning.

Using the metaphor of complexity theory, purpose becomes the attractor, like a lake in a basin, with all the behaviors in the organization acting as trajectories, following tributaries that drain into the lake. Purpose can be articulated at different levels. The grand or global purpose of an organism, survival, is the guiding beacon for behavior at the local levels where goals are achieved in support of the purpose, to further the cause of survival.

The concept of purpose is all-encompassing in the minding organization just as in the human body as an organism. The action-based creative leadership of the minding organization must focus on purpose at the global level to provide the context for actions at the local level. Purpose is an attractor that makes it possible to place our values and goals in a relevant context and to give meaning to our work at all levels, from the simplest menial tasks to the most sophisticated and challenging undertakings. The leadership of the minding organization must focus on the purpose of creating material value, but it must be always mindful of the need to cultivate social and spiritual values in the organization. Trust, truth, integrity, and loyalty (as discussed in Chapter 1) are central to the vitality of the minding organization.

The new leadership must be able to redefine a grand purpose in timely fashion as they listen to all sides of an issue, including the practical, theoretical, economical, legal, ethical, and moral, and balance the different forces that push and pull the organization in the turbulence of operating on the edge of chaos.

To achieve optimum performance, the new leaders must learn to reconcile conflicts and imbalances, and avoid the pitfalls of local optimization, namely going to extremes in one dimension at the expense of all others. The leaders must seek a balance that does justice to all dimensions in good measure, a sort of golden mean of the ideal state for the minding organization.

In what follows, we discuss purpose and value creation, the model of "all in good measure," its many applications, and its importance in the minding organization. We conclude with the anatomy of a problem that provides a model for achieving goals at the local level in the context of the higher-level purpose pursued by the minding organization. The application of the model is conditioned on leaders vesting people with the authority to make decisions at their level of work when the future unfolds and requires timely adaptation. The shared grand purpose of the organization, as articulated by the leadership, becomes the attractor that guides and gives meaning to the choices and actions at the local level throughout the organization.

Purpose in the Organization

Let us start with the assumption that human beings are purposeful creatures. We justify actions in the present because they contribute to results in the future. Although some actions lead to more immediate gratification, most results of our actions in the present have rewards in a more distant future. We are endowed with the ability to delay gratification but, nevertheless, invest resources of time, space, money, thought, and emotions in the present. Delayed gratification is a uniquely human capacity.

The resources of time, money, rational thinking, and emotions are limited. Therefore, we must choose from many alternative actions that compete for these limited resources. A grand strategy is needed to give a sense of purpose to our actions and provide direction to help us make decisions.

The model for the grand strategy is a quotient (Q), expressed as the ratio between value created (VC) and resources employed (R). This is expressed as follows: $Q = VC/R$.

The grand strategy is such that every member of the organization should act in a way that will increase VC/R. This is as broad as a grand strategy ought to be. However, to give the strategy meaning in the tactical choices at the local level of day-to-day work, we need to articulate the elements of VC/R in more detail.

The value created, VC, is for the entire organization. This value must be aligned with the value perceived by the individual. When such alignment exists, the individual will be driven to tap creativity to the greatest extent possible. If one of the key values in a minding organization is innovation, then people will use their brain power even to the point of making their current job obsolete.

The resources, R, which we use in the present, result in value created, VC, in the future. R can be measured. You can count the number of employees, you can count cash on hand, money in the bank, space available, or time. You can audit the

The New Leadership   153

intellectual property, count the number of patents issued, the number of people with advanced degrees, the laboratory facili ties, and the capacity for production. All these measurements are matters of fact that can be verified.

VC, which will unfold in the future, cannot be measured in the same way as R. Assessment of VC at the time R is commit- ted cannot be based on objective measurements. Assessment of VC, being in the future, cannot be based on fact and veri- fied at the present. VC is based on opinion and judgment, and as such, it is subjective and laden with uncertainty.

To increase $Q = VC/R$, we can proceed in a number of ways:

1. Increase VC and increase R.

2. Increase VC and hold R.

3. Increase VC and decrease R.

4. Hold VC and decrease R.

5. Decrease VC and decrease R.

VC can increase, decrease, or remain constant. So can R. Of the nine possible combinations, three will cause Q to decrease, one will keep it the same, and the five listed above will cause it to increase.

The efforts mounted by many organizations in recent years to restructure, reengineer, downsize, and contain costs have concentrated mostly on reducing R. Reduce expenditure, reduce the work force, reduce space used, reduce pay, reduce benefits, cut costs of production, negotiate reduction of sup- plier fees for parts and services, and so on. All these measures attempt to reduce R, not always considering whether the VC/R quotient will increase, remain constant, or decrease. Often, downsizing results in a reduction in VC/R, suggesting that the decrease in R causes a larger percent decrease in VC.

The prime reason for the focus on R is that it is easy to mea- sure. It is tangible and shows up immediately. You cut the workforce to one-half its former size, and you perceive an erro- neous improvement in VC/R. You believe that VC remains the same or it will be reduced by a smaller percentage than the reduction in R. However, the effect of the reduction in R is uncertain—it will unfold when the future becomes present.

The exclusive focus on R to improve VC/R is the wrong way to proceed. It proceeds from the present to the future. What we ought to do is work backward from the future to the present. Begin with VC and then assess a compatible level of R. This requires a heightened perception, a rich imagination, courage, creative thinking, and innovation, which force more chaos to the forefront. The more we do early on to consider the future, the more weight and leverage our actions carry to increase Q. This is shown schematically in Figure 8.1.

EXAMPLE

Consider chemical companies selling a solvent used in many industries. Competition is increasing and each company is looking for ways to improve.

Company X: Cost of transportation and delivery is reduced by designing a single-sized, 50-gallon container and instituting a new, more efficient vehicle for delivery.

Company Y: A companywide 10 percent cut in the workforce is mandated.

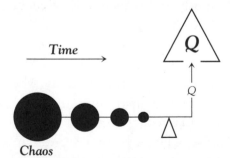

FIGURE 8.1 The more chaos there is at the beginning, the more order and quality there is at the end.

Company Z: Forces purchasing to negotiate new contracts with
suppliers with a minimum 15 percent reduction in costs.

While Companies X, Y, and Z are focusing on reducing R to
increase the quotient of VC/R, the Action-Based Creativity
Company (ABC) is focusing on both parts of the ratio—VC
and R. Teams of Company ABC live for a few days in the world
of the customer by arranging visits to select customers. They
focus on customers' needs and a potential competitive price for
their product. They ask the customers many questions and
return armed with perceptions, both from the customers and
their own, that may help them take action to shape a future
with an increase in VC/R for the customer and Company ABC.

In their visit, the teams observe, recognize, discover, and
learn of the key issues that can have serious effects on VC/R.
The customer wants availability of the chemical at all times,
without running out of stock. They also want a 15 percent
reduction in price to permit them to compete in the market of
their products.

Company ABC started from customer needs and found a creative way to increase VC/R for itself and the customer. They
negotiated new contracts with customers to make the chemical
available at all times without needing to place orders, wait for
deliveries, handle containers, receive invoices for quantities
purchased, nor initiate a purchase. Company ABC assumed the
role of managing the inventory of the chemical with no inter-
vention by the customer.

The creative approach resulted in a stainless steel tank
installed by Company ABC in the customer's plant. The customer draws the chemical from the tank on demand as needed.
A float with an attached electronic device measures the level
of chemical in the tank and calculates the amount used each
day. The information instructs a computer to transfer payment
electronically, for whatever quantity is used daily, from the customer's bank account to Company ABC's account. Company
ABC cut R by eliminating containers, billing, loading, and

unloading containers. Delivery trucks were replaced with tankers that replenish the fixed large tanks. The customer cut R by eliminating the need for placing orders, handling containers, storing them, and paying for unused inventory. It eliminated the cost of being out of stock. It received a reduction in price, and it collects a monthly rent for the large stainless steel tank that Company ABC keeps in its plant. The space is far smaller than that used to store the individual containers delivered in the old system. Company ABC has a five-year lease on the space for the tank with an option to renew for five more years. The price of the chemical was negotiated for a five-year period. A truly win-win arrangement for VC/R enhancement for all, in which Company ABC increased its market share and its VC/R at the same time.

The Model of "All in Good Measure"

The origin of the model of "all in good measure" can be traced to Aristotle, the Greek philosopher who was a pupil of Plato and teacher of Alexander the Great (384–322 B.C.). His contributions range from logic to ethics, from observations about the human brain to human character. He was one of the early contributors to the study of human nature and developed models of human conduct as it pertains to right and wrong. One of Aristotle's models of ethical behavior that has served as a guide to good conduct can be extended to many areas. The model says essentially that good character strives for the middle ground, and moves away from excess or exaggeration at either extreme. For example, in the matter of pride and shame, the middle ground is neither excessive arrogance nor excessive humility. In relations with other people, psychological maturity is to act in a way that is neither superior nor inferior to others. The general spirit of this model of conduct is a quest for the middle, the golden mean, a continuous search for the ideal state.

There are many phenomena in which a perpetual oscillation continues in the vicinity of an ideal state, or in the range of the optimum, searching for the middle ground between extreme opposites. Many of our bodily functions, such as control of body temperature, blood pressure, heart beat rate, hydrogen-ion concentration level, and calcium level in the blood are all governed by systems detecting departures from the ideal range and setting appropriate causes in motion to restore the range of the ideal state. These homeostatic conditions require constant vigilance by our self-regulating system and the use of negative feedback, causing a move to the right when the system veers to the left of the ideal, and a move to the left when it veers to the right of the ideal. These physical functions are automatic and involuntary.

We generalize this ideal and call it the model of "all in good measure," showing how it can serve the quest for relentless improvement. First we present the general model and then give a number of applications, concluding with its role in the minding organization.

"ALL IN GOOD MEASURE"

Figure 8.2 shows a general relationship between a cause, along the horizontal axis, and a resulting effectiveness (effect on performance), along the vertical axis. The objective is to move along the curve as closely as possible to the ideal (point T) which represents the highest level of effectiveness on the curve. Suppose the level of effectiveness is level P. This level is represented by two points on the curve, point A and point C. To achieve an increase in effectiveness from level P may require an increase or decrease in the cause, depending on whether we are at point A or point C on the curve, respectively. At point A the cause is at state a, and increasing it by a small amount results in a move from point A to point B on the curve and a corresponding increase in effectiveness from level P to level M (more). On the other hand, if we are at point C

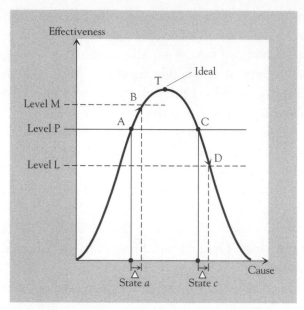

FIGURE 8.2 Relationship between cause and its resulting effect.

on the curve, then the cause is at state *c*, and increasing it by a
small amount results in a move from point C to point D on the
curve and a corresponding decrease in effectiveness from level
P to level L (less). Therefore, to increase effectiveness from
level P we must increase the cause at A and decrease it at C.

To achieve improvement, we must be vigilant and know
where we are on the curve when we are at level P. Are we at
point A or at point C? Often the way to find out is through
quick experimentation or trial and error, to determine whether
we must aim right or left, increase or decrease the cause. Once
we are close to the ideal point T, how do we continue our quest
for relentless improvement as a way of life? The answer lies in
the fact that most phenomena are influenced by multiple
causes that may exert their influences independently or depen-
dently. Thus, we can lift the entire curve of effectiveness versus cause upward and raise the effectiveness at all levels of one
cause by changing another.

EFFECTIVENESS AND TENSION

Figure 8.3 shows a relationship between effectiveness and human tension. The extremes of low and high tension result in low effectiveness. Each situation has an optimum range of tension for high levels of effectiveness close to the ideal level. At point A, more tension is warranted; at point C, relaxing tension is prudent. When we are overly relaxed, sluggish in our movements, and slow to respond with our mind (state *a* in the figure), our performance effectiveness can improve when we heighten our perception, thinking, and action by increasing tension at state *a*. On the other hand, with excessive tension (state *c* in the figure), our performance effectiveness can improve when we relax the tension.

EFFECTIVENESS AND TECHNOLOGY

Extremes in levels of technology, the old and outmoded at one end, the new or latest state of the art at the other end, may both result in low levels of effectiveness as shown in Figure 8.4. The move to the range of the optimum to increase effectiveness must be assessed by studying where the organization and its people are on the curve in terms of the ability to assimilate a

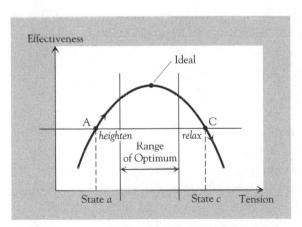

FIGURE 8.3 The relationship between effectiveness and tension.

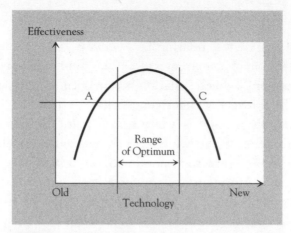

FIGURE 8.4 The relationship between new effectiveness and old technology.

sophisticated technology. For example, when bronze weapons were introduced, they were expensive to produce and could only be made available in small numbers. The Mycenaean Greek Civilization of the twelfth century B.C. (the Greek Bronze Age) adopted the new technology. The Dorians invaded the Mycenaeans and destroyed them. The Dorians succeeded because they were using simple, inexpensive iron swords of the old technology in large numbers against the highly developed and expensive bronze weapons of the Mycenaeans, which were in the hands of a relatively elite army.

GOVERNMENT REVENUES VERSUS TAXES

The Laffer Curve is a model of government revenues versus levels of income tax. At the extremes, we either pay no income tax or we are taxed at 100 percent. The good measure is somewhere in this range. Looking at Figure 8.5, at level L of revenues the question is whether we are at point A or point C on the curve. The errors occur when we wish to increase revenues above level L, and to achieve this we increase taxes at point C and decrease them at point A. Governments continue to

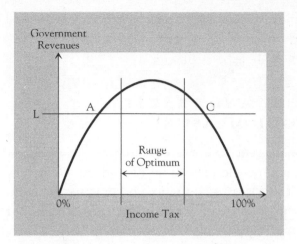

FIGURE 8.5 Government revenues versus income tax.

experiment, or engage in target practice, in a continuous quest to find the optimum zone, the good measure of income tax.

THE SEARCH FOR GOOD MEASURE IN IDEAL BEHAVIOR

In the realm of ethical behavior, the road to psychological maturity accompanied by personal integrity requires continued learning if we are committed to relentless improvement. To find the balance between humility and arrogance, independence and mature interdependence, giving and taking, leading and deferring leadership to others, selfishness and altruism requires a lifetime of trial and error, namely continued experimentation and target practice, and relentless search for the ideal behavior. To be alive and viable is never to stop searching for the good measures of ideal behavior. Even in our search for the truth, we must continue to seek the ideal. The intensity of our emotional commitment to the truth, as we perceive it, must be balanced by the truths held by others and by its contribution to justice and peace. There is a time to stand our ground and a time to yield. We must always remember the need to balance constancy and stability with flexibility and adaptability, a balance between preserving order and permitting the chaos of change, so we can continue the quest for improvement.

THEORY AND PRACTICE IN GOOD MEASURE

In the many years of work in industry and in academia we have often heard people refer to an idea as theoretical and, therefore, not practical, as if theory and practice are contradictory terms, the presence of one implying the absence of the other. The fact is that nothing is more practical than a sound theory. A theory is useful in explaining diverse phenomena and in unifying many fragments of experience that are disjointed and incoherent in the absence of theory. The theory that we have discussed here suggests that improvement often results from causes that are applied in good measure. Good measure is achieved as a result of a quest for a middle ground or level, away from the extremes of too little or too much. The model of "all in good measure" is a theory for applying causes in good measure. The applications that we have identified are only a small sample of a spectrum of applications. The applications can range from the search for improvement in the use of technology to the search for the ideal in personal integrity. It is a model characterized by its ubiquity. The model is the theory, and the application is the practice. Use theory and practice in good measure.

"All in Good Measure" in Organizations: The Body as a Metaphor

As an organism, the human body must keep many different functions in balance. The heart cannot decide that today it will take all the oxygen and let the spleen and liver get their own. All the parts need to cooperate and remain unified to ensure the survival of the total body. In a complex system, many factors must be balanced; attributes that, in and of themselves, may not seem important may in fact throw an entire system off if they are ignored. In any system, going to extremes is not beneficial. In the human organism, high blood pressure is bad, but so is low blood pressure; extreme obesity is bad, but so is anorexia. There is a midrange, which is optimal. This is counter to the notion that if something is good, then more is better. In complex systems, more may be counterproductive.

In an organization, various functions must also be kept in balance. Organizations tend to excel in and reward certain areas and deem other areas as auxiliary or secondary. If resources become scarce and secondary functions are dismissed, organizations may find themselves obsolete without understanding what has happened. By limiting their vision to a narrow field, the complex world tramples them. Committing the bulk of their efforts with too narrow a focus may eliminate them from future successes.

The organization's philosophy should be to pursue in depth a particular area of expertise, but to keep all eyes open on additional potential functions that can be adapted to the organization's innate abilities. At some point, the area of depth may need to be modified or altogether replaced, and an organization that has not prepared itself for adaptation will find itself in the same obsolescence as the dinosaur. For example, typewriter manufacturers that relentlessly improved typewriters wrote their own obituaries as word processing and personal computers were multiplying in the workplace.

To also be good at something else, a company must have a state of readiness. This is a skill that must be developed; peripheral vision must be practiced. Thus, companies that focus 100 percent of their efforts exclusively on an area of expertise are treading in dangerous waters.

The philosophy of "all in good measure" requires that we continuously ask ourselves whether we are overdoing efforts. Overdoing efforts results in diminishing returns or complete backfiring; the gap between what we desire and what transpires is our clue that we must reassess and regroup. Ask whether you are pushing too hard a technology or process that is on the last legs of its life. The only way to answer the question is to be on a continuous watch and quest for new knowledge, minding the technologies and processes that are becoming available.

The need for continuous monitoring is predicated on the reality that a company can excel in a field and be successful in a particular environment and reality. As environments change, however, excellence may become obsolete. The company may have been great for fulfilling a certain need, but needs change. Ice manufacturers provided a necessary and appreciated service until household refrigerators made them obsolete. The ice manufacturers were indispensable in one time frame but abandoned in the new reality. When you are the benchmark of the industry, it is even more devastating to find that the entire industry has been retired. It follows that everyone has to play the role of generalist, delving into peripheral, adjacent, or just plain interesting additional areas.

As discussed earlier in this book, we must learn to balance continuous ongoing improvement in a field of endeavor, namely evolution, with major and abrupt transitions to a new field, namely revolution. The period of time that we explore, monitor, and finally plunge into the new is the phase in the life of the organization that is on the edge of chaos at a very high level of intensity. This is shown in Figure 8.6. The transition from old to new, namely from ice making to refrigeration, from typewriters to word processors, from two-day delivery service to one-hour delivery, all these represent revolutions. Failure to make the phase transition from the old to the new precipitates the demise of an organization. It represents failure to adapt to change.

Achieving Local Goals While Pursuing Global Visions

The life of the organization on a day-to-day basis continues to evolve. Goals must be set and achieved at the local level while the organization is pursuing higher-level purposes. A useful

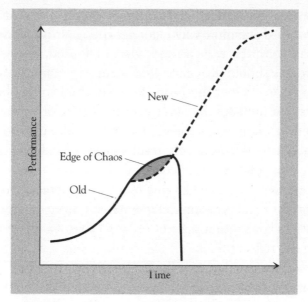

FIGURE 8.6 Edge of chaos: transition from old to new.

framework for solving problems at the local level is provided by the following anatomy of a problem.

Anatomy of a Problem

Problems that have any degree of complexity to them inherently start out in a state of chaos. The situation may be fuzzy and ill defined; it may not even be clear what exactly the problem is. In this ill-defined state, we lack a lot of details, and it may neither be clear how important the problem is nor what ramifications any solution may have. From this state of chaos, we must eventually bring the problem to a reasonable state of order, if we are going to deal with it.

All problems, whatever domain or content they deal with, share a similar anatomy. To begin thinking about any problem, the first step is to outline the skeleton of the problem. The basic elements of any problem are a context within which the problem is embedded, the present state, the goal state, and solutions to bridge the gap. The relationship between these elements is diagrammed in Figure 8.7. The initial state and goal state describe what is and what is desired, respectively. The process should articulate first what to do and only then how to do it. The entire problem is couched in the broader context that includes the purpose of the entire organization.

When we identify a problem, our first impulse is to do something about it. We are a very results-oriented culture, and we want to see solutions implemented. However, to effectively solve problems, we need to put more initial energy into the assessment of the problem's elements. We need to transform the initial chaos into a state of order so that we know we are solving the right problem.

Instead, we tend to engage in one-shot thinking, implementing the first solution that seems reasonable. People want to start working on solutions before it is clear what the present state is and which goal is ultimately desired. This is forward thinking (as opposed to thinking backward and more creatively)—"Let's implement a solution and if it doesn't work, we'll deal with those issues as they emerge." In other words, "We'll cross that bridge when we get there!" With this kind of thinking, there will be a need to undo and redo. There will be many costly errors made along the way, and people will waste their efforts having to constantly put out new fires.

Before thinking about solutions, we need to make sure that the present state of the problem and the goal state have been

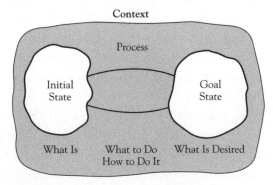

FIGURE 8.7 Anatomy of a problem.

given sufficient consideration. Each of them must be well defined before we try to bridge the gap with possible solutions. By spending some mental effort defining where we are and where we want to be, potential solutions will suggest themselves that otherwise never arise. The task of assessing which solution best bridges the gap should only be undertaken once the present and goal states are well defined. The question, then, is what makes for a well-defined problem. We use the acronym SMART to define characteristics of well-defined states.

SMART in the Present State

Consider first the present state of a problem. The attributes of a well-defined present state indicate that we have moved from the fuzzy state of chaos to a state of order in articulating the fact-based, present-state conditions of the problem.

<u>S</u>PECIFIC

The present state must be defined in terms of verifiable facts. To say, "We have personality problems in the office," is vague; to say, "My employees are unreasonable," is also vague. When somebody says, "We have safety problems to resolve," this, too, is vague. All of these statements must be more specific in terms of the facts to understand the present state. In terms of employees or personality problems, who is doing what to whom? How often? Who is suffering? In what way? If there are safety problems, what are they? Who is getting hurt? How badly? What is the nature of the injuries and what are the causes? To be specific, it is often helpful to describe the present state to an outsider who has no knowledge of the problem. To describe the problem to someone with no knowledge of your condition forces you to provide details, or the listener will not understand what you are talking about.

MEASURABLE

You need to be able to measure the present so that when you ultimately implement a solution, you will know if you are making any progress toward bridging the gap. Defining a problem in a measurable way may take some thinking. Your choice of yardstick for measurement will serve as part of the definition of the problem, and will determine the kinds of solutions you consider.

If you work with a team and complain that they do not work fast enough, this is not yet measurable. To say that they take five days to do a two-day project is measurable. Suppose your problem is lack of job safety. How will you measure this present state? Number of workers injured? The cost to the company in lost production? Public perception of your company? Each of these measures defines the problem differently and will influence the type of solutions considered.

ACCURATE

Accuracy refers to the truth of the facts defining the present state. Assumptions and premises may be taken for granted but completely wrong. In addition, information enhanced with a lot of details might be assumed to be accurate, when, in fact, details ensure neither correctness nor truth. The information may be precise, but we should not confuse precision with accuracy.

REASONABLE AND RELEVANT

In an assessment of the present state we have to be reasonable in determining the facts; we don't want to overdo any fact-finding mission. This brings us to an issue of balance. We need facts and they need to be accurate, but there comes a point of diminishing returns—we need to question whether additional facts will add value. Namely, will added information make a relevant difference in our assessment of the present state?

TRACKABLE

The present state is dynamic; it continuously changes as we make progress toward the goal. It is critical to vigilantly assess where we are in relation to where we have been and where we want to be, to know if we are making timely progress toward the goal. Tracking the present state keeps us alert to changes that may require quick adaptations and midcourse corrections as the future becomes the present.

SMART in the Goal State

Now let us consider the goal state. Unlike the present, which is based on facts, the goal state is in the future. As such, it requires judgment, opinion, intuition, and hunches. The future is not fact until it unfolds and becomes the present. Therefore, the future is difficult to verify and the attributes of a well-defined goal state differ somewhat from those of the present state. Nevertheless, the SMART acronym is still viable as a definition.

SENSE OF PURPOSE

Before embarking on the achievement of any goal, we should first establish how fulfilling the goal fits in with our overall sense of purpose. A sense of purpose defines a general direction we are striving for; particular goals fit in this framework as strategies for achieving the general sense of purpose. Without considering a goal within the larger context of purpose, we may end up solving the wrong problem or creating new ones that move us away from our overriding purpose.

MEANINGFUL

Can you envision addressing an issue that serves no purpose? Goals vary in how meaningful they are—namely, how well they serve the sense of purpose. Is the goal meaningful in the context of the entire organization? The goal must serve the ultimate purpose of the entire organization for it to have meaning.

ALIGNED AND ACHIEVABLE

Is the goal considered achievable and is it aligned with all of the other goals you have? Is the goal of your department aligned with the larger, company goals? If a company wants to cut costs, it may be unwise to tell all departments to cut costs—this may result in each department taking actions that are not aligned with the broader company goal. For example, if a department supervisor knows that her accounting books are checked every month for wasteful spending, and she finds a way to save $150 in employee travel per diem expenses, this may actually cost the company thousands of dollars in higher plane ticket costs because the employees are flying more expensive morning flights to save hotel bills. Because the supervisor is not checked for flight expenses, only for per diem expenses, her goal to cut her department's costs actually work against the larger company goal of saving money. The proverb "penny wise, pound foolish" reflects goals that are not aligned.

REALISTIC

Some goals may be achievable, but they are neither realistic nor reasonable. Suppose that personality problems in your office are such that nobody is on speaking terms. A possible goal would be to create a one-person operation and fire everyone else. But is this realistic? Can you do all the work by yourself? Or, perhaps you don't want to rely on outside partners and would prefer complete vertical integration, from raw material to final product. In today's world, this is not realistic when competitors are outsourcing jobs to others who can do the work faster and cheaper.

TIMELY

Is the goal stated in such a way that the target must be achieved within some time frame? Deadlines are important; people tend to start working toward a goal with much more effort once the halfway point has been reached. If a goal is two years down the road, most of the effort is put forth after one year. To overcome this handicap, it helps to set subgoal deadlines—the one-year goal, the six-month goal, the one-month goal, and even the seven-day goal. These subgoal deadlines can best be created by working backward from the end goal. Like the ultimate goal, the subgoals need to also be defined by SMART.

The minding organization requires a new leadership that generates action-based creativity at all levels of work. To this end, the leadership must balance in good measure its responses to the forces of turbulence in an environment of ongoing chaos. It must articulate a grand purpose to provide a context for distributed decision making at all levels at which the future unfolds and timely adaptation is required.

The Minding
Organization in Action

The Minding
Organization in Action

It is always thrilling to hear from former students, and get their stories about how the ideas discussed in this book are applicable to their real-world problems or problems they hear about. In June 1997, Ronald Orr from TRW e-mailed an article published in *Wired* magazine, entitled "Bordering on Chaos," by Peter Katel. The article describes the transformation of a subsidiary of Cementos Mexicanos (Cemex for short) located in Guadalajara, Mexico, and is a perfect example of the application of the ideas described in this book.

Cemex is at present the world's third-largest concrete company. It employs over 20,000 people, has close to 500 plants, thousands of vehicles, ships, and communication satellites linking operations in over 60 countries. The annual revenues generated per employee are close to $150,000, about the same as those for a major aerospace giant of 200,000 employees in the United States. These revenues are generated from ready-mix concrete, a commodity, not a sophisticated, aerospace, state-of-the-art technology or innovative product.

The transformation began when the company was going through a very difficult period economically. The operations of the ready-mix business were troubled by the uncertainties of meeting delivery schedules. More than two-thirds of the deliveries were not on time. Reasons varied: Customers might not be ready, trucks were lost en route or delayed by traffic and weather. There were more people calling the company to complain about late orders than people calling to place new orders for concrete. It was then that the company executives decided to take the plunge and put complexity theory to work. They transformed the company into a self-organizing system that embraces chaos and uncertainty, and learns to thrive in an environment that unfolds so quickly, no rigid, advanced planning could possibly anticipate and respond to it.

There were two central issues: uncertainty and the future. The future, of course, is less uncertain and more possible to predict when it is closer to the present. The question then was: How could the company organize to bring the future closer to the present? How could concrete be delivered just in time, when needed, with an order placed one hour in advance, not scheduled one or two days in advance. The future is, indeed, closer to the present when delivery is only one hour away from the order. What would the company look like in the future if it could do this? Cemex executives needed to get a glimpse of the future and see their company responding to customer needs as they emerged, following random sequences of times and places, in a chaotic world of concrete ready-mix orders.

Cemex found a way to visit the future. Cemex teams first visited one of the sites of Federal Express, a company that delivers within 24 hours, and were impressed by the impeccability of the service. Then they had a bolder and more provocative thought. They visited the 911 operation of fire and ambulance services in a major U.S. city. After all, nobody calls 911 to request service 24 hours in advance; when a call comes in, the emergency is not in the future, it is in the present. This was the model they were looking for; this would be the future of their ready-mix concrete company.

After several months of effort within the entire organization, with all employees involved in the process of adapting, the company was transformed. Each ready-mix truck driver and his truck is now an independent, autonomous decision maker, cruising the city in certain regions of new construction, waiting for an order. An on-board computer puts each truck in contact with other trucks and with the single center for operations where orders come in. A global positioning sensor in each truck makes it possible to know and track its position. Each truck driver now communicates unfolding events on the road, such as accidents, traffic jams, and weather conditions. The information helps the system of trucks cruising the city adapt to the world of unplanned occurrences, to respond to that which cannot be anticipated by a plan in advance.

The trucks now cruise the city in a configuration that changes from week to week and, at times, from day to day. The pattern of cruising for any given week is a result of conversations by the drivers in which their human judgments are combined with facts from a computer database that tracks newly issued building permits, new construction, and other relevant facts. The adaptive-learning computer program that helps in adapting a cruising plan for the trucks is light-years away from the previous losing battle of trying to adhere to a rigid delivery schedule planned in advance. The random distribution of trucks in the city adapts to the random distribution of incoming orders from construction sites in the city. The computer program of truck distribution and cruising is augmented by on-the-spot, just-in-time decisions by the driver who decides which options to exercise. The site of an order might be only a 15-minute drive away from a cruising truck, based on the computer display of the city map and the location of the truck and building site. If the truck driver perceives a problem, however, such as a traffic accident that will impede his progress, he can call for another truck or alert the central operations room.

Delivery can thus still be made on time by another truck—or it might be impossible to deliver on time. In a world in which you embrace uncertainty and chaos, you cannot please all of the customers all of the time, but you must continue to pay attention to every customer some of the time, and be relentless about improvement.

A single operations room for the entire city replaced the order takers and dispatchers in each of the plants. The operations room is equipped with six telephone lines, five computer screens, and two human operators. One of the large screens is a city map. On this screen, the site of an incoming order is located instantaneously as well as the locations of trucks within range for delivery within the requested amount of time. This data can be augmented by driver judgment once the order is relayed to the trucks within range. The financial billing status of the customer is checked even before the customer hangs up. In addition, recordings of all incoming and outgoing calls are kept. Computer programs are updated on an ongoing basis. This includes truck maintenance, cruising patterns, construction status, road conditions, and weather predictions. A learning, adapting program is augmented by the power of human judgment.

Within a year, company on-time deliveries reached 98 percent. The company provides a 25 percent discount for concrete delivered more than 20 minutes late. Cemex advertises its commitment to speedy, on-time delivery by distributing miniature pizza boxes with the slogan, "Now concrete is delivered faster than pizza."

The Cemex revolution did not create breakthrough technology; rather, it used existing technology to deliver a commodity of ready-mix concrete. Computers, communication satellites, and local area and wide area networks are used to link Cemex operations in the 60 countries in which it now operates. There is much more to the story than a short account can describe. Issues include adjusting to a new culture; spreading the risk of doing business by going global; and instituting a learning organization in the company with in-house education, training, and incentives for back-to-school degree programs. The emergence of networks of people to augment company hierarchies makes it possible to embrace a companywide commitment to excellence through three *p*s: articulation of *p*urpose, making a *p*romise, and the bottom line of *p*erformance to deliver on the promises that serve the purpose.

The Thirteen Precepts of the Minding Organization

The transformation process of Cemex embodies the main elements of the message of this book. An organization can become a thriving, coevolving, adapting organism. Such an organization lives by the following 13 precepts. These precepts embody the brain, heart, and soul of the minding organization.

Precept 1: The CEO is transformed into an OEC, from chief executive officer in a rigid hierarchy of organizational charts to an operator on the edge of chaos in a flexible, evolving, ever-renewing network of relationships internal to the company and external to it, with customers, suppliers, competitors, and allies.

Precept 2: To tap creativity, innovation, and achieve successful business solutions, plan some activities and permit the rest to evolve. Aim for a target of 50/50; 50 percent planned and 50 percent unplanned. Learn to work from chaos to order.

Precept 3: Commit to relentless improvement through ongoing cycles of chaos to order, balancing revolution with evolution.

Precept 4: Learn to think backwards: kniht.

Precept 5: Cultivate people, the only resource that can find meaning in purpose, and use commitment, judgment, and intuition to transform an organization into an organism, a minding organization.

Precept 6: Embrace uncertainty; neither fight it nor try to impose order on it. Adapt to it. Coevolve with the forces of the environment.

Precept 7: Pay attention to every customer. By necessity, ignore some of the customers some of the time.

Precept 8: Permit networks to evolve within and outside the organization.

Precept 9: Distribute decision making to where the future unfolds. Give workers the knowledge and skills they need to do their job. Vest people with the authority to be wrong coupled with a commitment to a shared purpose that becomes the attractor, that gives meaning to choices and actions at the local level.

Precept 10: Bring the future to the present. Whenever possible, visit the future.

Precept 11: Balance the quantitative data, facts, and logic with human qualitative judgments, intuition, and fertile imagination.

Precept 12: Use optimism, diversity, and errors as strategies.

Precept 13: Cultivate mutual trust and respect. Only trust can release the full potential for creativity and innovation, and permit the human spirit to soar.

EPILOGUE

Figure E.1 is a plot of the world's population in the last 2,000 years. The circles on the curve show the span of time for the population to double in size. It took 1,200 years for the population to double in size from 200 million people to 400 million. It will take only 40 years for the population to double in size from 3 billion to 6 billion. Contemplate the implications of the transitions. Complexity theory will be in action everywhere. This is something to think about as we start a new millennium and adopt a new metaphor for the organization.

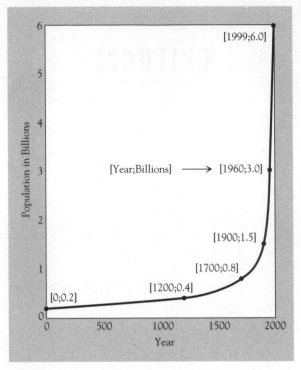

FIGURE E.1 Accelerated exponential growth of the world's population.

APPENDIX

From Pyramids to Computers

A BRIEF HISTORY OF MANAGEMENT AND THE RISE OF THE AGE OF THE BRAIN

Imhotep

About 4,700 years ago, an engineer named Imhotep orchestrated the design and construction of one of the most amazing structures of all times—the great pyramid in Giza, near Cairo, Egypt. The pyramid has a square base measuring 756 feet on each side. The four triangular faces meet at the apex of the structure, 480 feet above the base of the pyramid. The base is oriented in north-south and east-west directions within one-tenth of a degree, a precision of 0.03 percent. The pyramid consists of 2,300,000 blocks of stone with an average weight of two and one-half tons each. It took 20 years to complete, with slave labor numbering 100,000 at times. How did Imhotep raise those heavy stones to such heights as construction progressed? Imhotep did it all with simple tools, lots of slaves, and a brain that had the capacity for creativity that matches those of the best minds of our times.

The Egyptians were not concerned with short-term results of quarterly corporate reports. They were obsessed with the afterlife, hence their focus on burial places, which the pyramids were, and in which they placed their household goods as well as the servants to serve them in the world to come. Imhotep thus had lots of time to do the work. However, he had little information by today's standards, and what information did exist was not readily accessible.

Today, in the age of computers, we have the opposite end of the spectrum when it comes to time, information, and accessibility. We have chronically little time to do a task, we have lots of information, and we have a staggering number of channels of connectivity to access information at fantastic speeds.

Imhotep treated his manpower strictly as labor. Obedience and compliance were expected, demanded, and obtained with little regard for dignity or life. Imhotep, with possibly a small cadre of helpers, did the thinking and brain work for everybody. Imhotep was the one man in control of the flow of work as construction of the pyramid progressed.

Although a lot changed from the days of Imhotep to the days when the industrial revolution was in full force, the command and control of the assembly line was similar in many ways. The emphasis was on productivity through division of labor in the production process. Work was divided into simple, repetitive tasks in shaping a part or product on the assembly line so that little training and no thinking were required to perform a task. A small cadre of people in control did the thinking and brain work for everybody.

We now briefly trace the history of management science, starting with a story that goes back to 1776, and ends with the current age of computers. We shall note the transition from the focus on manual work to brain work, from productivity and efficiency to creativity and innovation expected from everybody.

Division of Labor

In 1776, a revolution of sorts took place. At that time, there lived seven carpenters in Boston. Each carpenter was an artisan with a small workshop, handcrafting chairs for individual customers on a made-to-order basis. One day, one of the carpenters got hold of a new book entitled *The Wealth of Nations* by a Scottish political economist and philosopher named Adam Smith (1723–1790). As he read, he was struck by an exciting application of an idea articulated in the book. He conceived a new, provocative, and revolutionary work plan to share with his colleagues. The following Sunday he gathered the other six carpenters to reveal his plan. Instead of each artisan working in a separate workshop making an integrated complete chair, they would jointly operate from a large workspace and fragment the work of making a chair. The anatomy of a chair, composed of a seat, back, two front legs, two back legs, and armrests, would be divided among them. One carpenter would spend his days making nothing but seats, another making only armrests, and so on, with one specialized task for each of the six carpenters. They would be located around the room, and in the center the seventh carpenter would work, assembling the parts into chairs. He would walk around the room with a cart to collect pieces, then take them to create the final product at a fixed station in the center of the workspace. They all agreed that if at any time there were enough of one particular part and not enough of another, they would help each other out until they could synchronize their efforts. In time, they would be able to supply the center assembly station with just the right number of chair parts at the rate at which they could be assembled.

The carpenters agreed that this plan was ingenious; it would allow each to work less and achieve more, and so the plan was implemented. Almost immediately, they realized that some of their habitual work strategies would have to change. For example, as they spewed out parts, the carpenter in charge of final assembly was spending too much time trying to identify parts that fit together, and making adjustments in the parts that did not fit. They realized that they would have to standardize the parts to make the final assembly flow more smoothly.

Thus, the first rule of the division of labor was standardization. In the past, a carpenter creating a chair in its entirety could maneuver and adjust as the need developed, and every chair was a little different from any other chair that had been created. Now, in the name of efficiency, sameness was the operating adjective. Because no single carpenter would have control over a chair, the process now dictated the way each would have to perform their task. The result was not only standardization of the final product, but standardization of the process, and consequently, of individual workers.

The benefit of the division of labor was an immediate marked increase in productivity. The carpenters were thrilled that at the end of a workday they could look at a room full of chairs, knowing that, working alone, such an output would have taken them days to achieve. In addition, they were impressed at how uniform and identical the chairs were, an accomplishment they had never seen before. Because they could lower the price of chairs, the carpenters saw customers in numbers previously unheard of, and they were euphoric.

After a few months, one of the seven cut his finger while sawing a chair leg. His mind had drifted and he wasn't paying attention to the job. He complained to his fellow craftsmen that it was boring to make chair legs day after day. They all reluctantly agreed that their tasks were also boring, and they concluded that it just wasn't as exciting and satisfying to create a chair anymore. Each of their chairs used to be different and could accommodate the individual tastes of customers; each craftsman could take pride in his accomplishment. Now the carpenters had no contact with customers, all the chairs were alike, and there was not the same feeling of pride as before.

The division of labor as the carpenters practiced it was the beginning of the industrial revolution. The carpenters had created the beginning of an organization, a system of sharing resources in the name of productivity. The identifying characteristic was sameness. For division of labor to work within the organization, an era of sameness took hold. Sameness in output as a result of sameness in input. Discipline in the workplace became a primary concern. If, in the past, workers could progress at their own pace, now a worker had to keep up with the speed dictated by the process and maintain the standards needed to assemble the final product. If a worker took a break, others who depended on his output would be stranded. So work hours, rest breaks, and output became highly regulated and disciplined. Individual needs had to be suppressed.

The Assembly Line

In the 1820s, transportation was revolutionized with the advent of railroads. People could now travel long distances with greater ease. However, what the railroads did was an extension of the era of sameness. With a horse and buggy, a traveler could go in any direction, at the time of their own choosing, at any pace they desired. With railroads, people could travel only between fixed points, on the same track, based on a dictated timetable. The system was highly structured and had to be extremely disciplined. Initially, only a single pair of railroad tracks ran in any direction so two trains coming from opposite directions had to share the same tracks but somehow avoid colliding. Sidetracks were installed for one train to pull in and wait for an opposing train to pass. For this to work, train timetables had to be rigidly enforced. The organization of the railroads required discipline, synchronization, and uniform behavior by all involved.

Railroads created the need for complex, monolithic organizations whose survival depended on sameness, with no latitude for maneuverability in the literal, as well as the organizational, sense. This was the beginning of the corporate command-and-control hierarchy, with focused but very limited tasks for each individual worker, and the thinking done at the top of the hierarchy by very few.

Henry Ford—Command and Control

At the beginning of the twentieth century, another event revolutionized society—the introduction of the automobile. In one sense, this was a return to the horse-and-buggy days; people could travel at any time, to any location, at any pace. This was a return to flexibility.

Henry Ford saw this new potential for personal mobility as a great opportunity. Unlike others of his time who viewed the automobile as a tool for the rich, Ford wanted to create a car for regular folks. Ford's philosophy was to keep it simple. He designed a single model, which a customer could get in any color they wanted—as long as it was black. (Actually, Ford's first cars came in a variety of colors. However, later, when speed of production intensified, all cars were painted black, because black enamel dried faster than the other colors.)

With the industrial revolution already widespread, Ford set up automobile manufacturing. Not only did he have a product that revolutionized the way people lived, Ford's methods and the ways in which he modified accepted production strategies revolutionized the way we do business.

Assembly of previously made parts was already normal production protocol, going back to our carpenters. Ford created a better way to mass-produce products with the assembly line. The assembly line fragmented the heretofore integrated task of putting pieces together to form the finished product. Instead of assembling parts into the final product at a fixed workstation, Ford had the parts move to stationary workers, each one contributing a fragment to the final assembly. Perhaps Ford was influenced by the model of a train moving along tracks, because his assembly model had the same structure. Just as trains stopped at fixed stations and people got on or off, Ford's cars moved down a line, and at fixed stations, parts were added or modified. At the end of the line, a complete car emerged. The process was synchronized and demanded adherence to a rigid timetable, just like the trains.

The revolution in thinking was just as profound as the revolution in process—there was no integrated final assembly as there was in the carpenters' workplace. Each worker contributed to a fragmented final assembly. The concept of dividing manual work to produce parts was applied to the assembly of the parts. This removed workers yet another step from mindful understanding and pride of creation.

Ford was so successful that cars were sold as quickly as they could be produced. Getting workers who could meet his growing demands, however, became a problem. Workers needed to be trained, and many were not educated. In fact, many were new immigrants who did not speak English. To compound the problem, turnover was enormous, over 370 percent in 1913. People tired of the monotonous drudgery of the mindless assembly process. To reduce turnover, Ford decided to shape workers in the image of the organization as he saw it.

The organization of the twentieth century would create an image and mold workers into that image. The complex assembly of pieces could not be disturbed with uncertainty emanating from the workforce. Ford viewed the worker the same way he viewed any other part of the automobile: It had to be standardized, uniform, predictable, and meet predetermined quality levels. Just as materials were inspected before being used, Ford inspected workers before they were hired. Prospective employees were interviewed at home and were judged for cleanliness, sober living, clean language, and other factors that Ford thought would affect their productivity. Once hired, workers were indoctrinated in the Ford philosophy and shaped in the company image much like raw steel was molded into a wheel axle. At the same time, workers were given benefits unheard of outside the industry. In 1914, Ford cut the workday from nine hours to eight, and increased salaries from two and one-half dollars to five dollars a day. Considering that New York City police officers were earning about three dollars a day,

Ford's compensation package was extremely generous and attracted a large pool of employees. Part of Ford's strategy was to pay his workers enough to afford a car—and once a worker had a car, everyone in his neighborhood would want a car—so he viewed these high salaries as good business.

Complete Control–Vertical Integration

Ford became so obsessed with control that he extended his reach beyond the manufacture of the car and the lives of his workers. He wanted to control the entire genesis of his every need, and refused to rely on suppliers. He bought thousands of acres of hardwood forests in Michigan to secure the lumber he needed, as well as lumber-processing plants, iron mines, steel mills, glass-making factories, rubber plantations in Brazil, and ships for transporting goods and materials. By buying all the suppliers that created the links in the chain, from raw materials to finished products, Ford was able to exert complete vertical control. His distrust of any organization outside his own was so intense that Ford Motor Company kept all its money in a vault at the plant, not in a bank. When Henry Ford II took over the company in 1945, the vault contained $700 million in cash!

Control of the Customer

The industrial revolution in general, and Ford's complete control specifically, resulted in a virtual dictatorship in terms of what would be available to the customer. Instead of a customer giving a craftsman specifications to incorporate in a product, the corporation was now giving the customer two choices— take it or leave it! Custom work became very expensive. This was a profoundly different way of doing business. It changed the fabric of society; as everyone drove the same car and wore the same mass-produced clothing, mass production created the era of sameness through customer control.

Corporate Divisions, Specialization, and Fragmentation

As the industrial revolution continued, so did specialization and fragmentation. General Motors initiated the concept of divisions within the parent organization. New departments like Marketing and Sales were created, and the role of the general manager was introduced to oversee all the separate divisions. Other organizations soon followed suit. From an organizational framework, workers were getting further and further away from each other and away from the core. People across divisions did not work together, and to an extent, even competed with one another for the company's resources. The core of the organization, the parent head at the top, was completely removed from all the divisions and was an entity unto itself. Quite a reach from the seven carpenters working as an organization. With every seeming advance in corporate structure, the employee was becoming a less-viable, integrated, integral part of the core.

The division of manual work into separate tasks and the division of brain work into narrow specialties dominated the structure of every institution created in the twentieth century. Services such as hospitals, educational entities, and government all evolved in this framework. Dividing, specializing, and fragmenting were the key structural elements. In the name of efficiency, this was a way to get more for time, money, and other limited resources. One of the immediate consequences of fragmentation for industry was a lack of communication across divisions, creating problems previously unknown. Manufacturing would have no idea what Marketing was doing, Engineering and Manufacturing would have no idea what Maintenance needed for its task. Each simply passed their contribution to the department responsible for the next phase in the process. Presumably, there was someone at the top of the organization who had "the big picture," but if there indeed was such a vision, it never filtered down through the hierarchy, nor was it shared across divisions.

Organization and Structure

The most commonly known organizational structure is the functional organization with a chief executive officer (CEO) presiding over separate departments, such as design, engineering, manufacturing, sales, finance, and research. In more recent years, additional departments have been created, such as planning, human resources, customer relations, and information systems. The departments in the functional organization cannot exist on their own. The CEO must ensure that a coordinated effort is in place for the departments to integrate their separate contributions to the whole.

The form of the fragmentation has changed over the years. Nevertheless, division and fragmentation characterize all of the forms. Some forms keep divisions completely isolated from each other as separate operating units, or profit centers in entirely different businesses, from toy making to insurance and cosmetics. Such an organization may be a holding company that, from relatively small headquarters, controls the financial life of the separate companies it holds or owns. In a holding company, each division is a company. Other forms, such as a multidivisional organization, share resources such as sales, marketing, and possibly research and development across divisions, but the concept of division is always at the forefront. Even in the matrix organization format, in which individuals from different functions become part of a project team, each employee has a "home," a function to which he or she returns at the completion of the project.

Scientific Management

The scientific management movement was introduced in the early 1900s by one of the first and best-known management gurus of all times, Frederick Winslow Taylor (1856–1915). Taylor became famous when he was retained by a Boston lawyer named Louis D. Brandeis, who later became a Supreme Court Justice, to help him argue a case against a railroad rate increase before the Interstate Commerce Commission. With the help of Taylor's scientific management theories, it was argued that the railroads could save more than $1 million a day by improving effectiveness through scientific management models, and thus no rate increase was warranted. Brandeis won the case and the publicity made Taylor famous and his theories better known.

From 1898 until 1901, Taylor worked at the Bethlehem Steel Company in Pennsylvania. Taylor introduced many innovations that improved effectiveness and efficiency of men and machines. One of those innovations emerged from a study of shoveling. Taylor noticed that the workers, who did work with shovels at Bethlehem, owned their own shovels. They brought their shovels along to work and used them for any job, be it moving coal, sand, gravel, or iron ore. Taylor decided to find the ideal load in pounds for a shovel.

The ideal shovel load was found to be 21.5 pounds for any shovel and any material moved. Using this model, shovel scoops were designed for this capacity, and as a result the average amount of material moved per man per day increased from 16 tons to 59 tons. Average earnings per worker increased by 60 percent.

Taylor then set out to raise productivity even higher. He turned his attention to the shape of the shovel and the shoveling process. He became obsessed with efficiency to the point that the judgments of the worker were replaced by predetermined uniform and repetitive movements at a pace entirely controlled by means external to the worker. In the name of efficiency, the worker was being reduced to a machine.

Taylor's analytic approach that ushered the beginning of scientific management led to the study of time and motion and continued to evolve with new themes every decade.

In the 1930s, Elton Mayo of the Harvard Business School, who conducted the Hawthorne experiments in the Western Electric Company, started to focus on the human and social problems of an industrial civilization. Human relations, motivation, and the psychology of work were in vogue in the 1930s.

The 1940s and World War II introduced operations research with its emphasis on quantitative analytical mathematical models of problems in organizations. This development coincided with the appearance of the electronic computer to permit the extensive computation required in the application of large-scale mathematical models of linear, nonlinear, and dynamic programming.

The 1950s expanded the analytical tools of management into systems analysis, in the study of large-scale systems, and set the stage for tools of the 1960s, such as the critical path method (CPM) for scheduling complex activities, program evaluation review techniques (PERT), and industrial dynamics using control theory, namely cybernetic feedback models.

In the 1970s, strategic planning and forecasting became the focus of attention, only to be overshadowed by the obsession with the quality movement. Quality circles, statistical process control, and total quality management were the terms and issues of the day in the 1980s. Reengineering, reinventing the corporation, downsizing, right-sizing, and flat organization are the in-words in the 1990s.

The harnessing of energy with the invention of the steam engine, and the machine age that followed, made it possible to amplify human muscles through the use of machines. As we enter the twenty-first century, human toil in the form of the blue-collar worker of the industrial age is disappearing at an ever-increasing rate and is being replaced by machines. The need for unskilled labor is constantly on the decrease. Demand for skilled labor to augment machines is on the increase.

The harnessing of information with the advent of the computer, and the information age that ensued, has made it possible to amplify human cognitive abilities. The clerical information-processing work of the white-collar worker is being taken over at an increasing rate by the computer. Routine repetitive clerical work by humans is on the decrease. Demand for knowledge workers to augment the computer is on the increase. Thus, only trained skilled workers can use machines in a productive way in the new age, and only educated knowledge workers can use computers in a productive way in the new age.

Computers and Communication

Computers and communication technologies, from satellites to fax machines, and cellular phones coupled with global positioning sensors, have ushered in the latest revolution, the information age. Mass production and sameness is giving way to mass customization. In manufacturing, the assembly line of the past meant fixed facilities and reliance on the sameness of mass production and economies of scale of long production runs for large lots of the same product. Flexible manufacturing makes it possible now to reconfigure production facilities such that any lot size is feasible and profitable. Diversity replaces sameness as each product can be specified to the needs of different customers, thus rapidly serving a variety of customers. Information age technology makes it possible to deliver parts, such as seats for a car, to a location on the assembly line where they are needed, just in time for them to be installed. This reduces the need for inventory and inventory control. Decision making can be delayed and made just in time. Clothing, bicycles, eyeglasses, and many other products are mass customized on a scale that rivals the heyday of mass production. A customer can literally visit the future before a choice is made. You can see yourself on a screen with virtually an unlimited number of frames for eyeglasses. Hairstyles can be tried on in the same fashion, before a single hair on your head is cut.

Traditional postal mail is replaced by electronic mail, making communication instantaneous. The Internet creates a network that makes it possible for us to access information sources on a global scale. The most amazing aspect of the Internet is that nobody is in charge! Other systems have some form of authority, and there is some form of hierarchy in almost every other type of organization. Coaches, captains, bosses, supervisors, parents, teachers—all of these are positions of control. The Internet comprises loosely connected parts that work— and nobody is in control. It forces us to rethink what is necessary to make a system work.

Computers Are Not Always the Solution

Following an invitation by the Chinese government to visit China, Moshe found himself mired in the process of obtaining a visa. Despite the fact that he was officially invited, the process involved six months of persistent delays. Here is how the system works. A visa application is completed and goes to a clerk who specializes in receiving such forms. The file is then passed on to the next specialist, a security clerk, who checks the applicant's background for any possible criminal record. Anything that appears questionable may be cause for delay as the record is investigated more thoroughly. Once this is done, the file moves to a health specialist who screens the applicant's medical history, checking that contagious diseases will not be brought into the country. The next specialist is an economist who looks into the reasons for the applicant's visit—business or pleasure. A political agent may be the next specialist poring over the file, checking for political affiliations, and then on to yet another specialist in consular affairs, who decides the duration of the visit and what type of visa to issue. Finally, the file moves to the dispensing department, which sends the applicant the visa. When everything is said and done, there is a single stamp on a solitary page, which takes six months to obtain.

Suppose a computer consultant is brought in to improve the efficiency of the existing process at the consulate. Each of the functions can be analyzed, with some paperwork eliminated and consolidated at each of the stations, and computers brought in to improve information flow. Each of the fragments can be made more efficient with the consultant able to cut each clerk's time spent with the file. If an uncomplicated file required 60 minutes from each clerk, the efficiency expert is able to cut that time to 10 minutes—a remarkable savings from the clerk's point of view. Because there are six clerks, a file that required six hours can now be completed in one hour, a savings of five hours. What has been gained by the applicant? Instead of getting the visa in six months, the visa will be available in six months minus five hours!

Because brain work has been as fragmented as manual work, people have lost the pride and sense of responsibility that goes along with ownership of a project, be it as simple as issuing a visa, making a chair, or more complex projects. The effect of such fragmented brain work ultimately affects the customer and their relation with the company. How often do you call a company and get transferred from one person to another, because your request does not fit the listener's job description? The technological mirror of such phone transfers comes in the shape of answering machines that ask you to press 1 if you need so-and-so, press 2 for such-and-such, with the result that you never actually speak to a human being, and you can only get information that has been anticipated in advance. Neither of these systems gets much praise from consumers.

The twenty-first century is introducing a new age to management science. It is the age of the brain. It is the age of finding ways to tap more of the human potential for creativity and innovation, and an ongoing guidance of the mind to a sense of purpose and meaning in our personal and professional lives.

SOURCES

Adizes, Ichak. *How to Solve the Mismanagement Crisis*. Homewood IL: Dow Jones-Irwin, 1979.

Batten, Mary. *Discovery by Chance: Science and the Unexpected*. New York, NY: Funk and Wagnalls, 1968.

Collins, Robert C. *Neurology*. Philadelphia, PA: W.B. Saunders Company, 1997.

De Camp, L. Sprague. *The Ancient Engineers*. New York, NY: Ballantine Books, 1974.

Frankl, Viktor E. *The Will to Meaning*. Harmondsworth, Middlesex, England: New American Library, 1970.

Gardner, Howard. *Frames of Mind: The Theory of Multiple Intelligences*. New York, NY: Basic Books, 1983.

Gordon, Thomas. *Parent Effectiveness Training*. New York, NY: New American Library, 1975.

Hardin, Garrett. *Filters Against Folly*. New York, NY: Penguin Books, 1986.

Jones, Charlotte Foltz. *Mistakes that Worked*. New York, NY: Doubleday, 1991.

Kauffman, Stuart. *At Home in the Universe*. New York, NY: Oxford University Press, 1995.

Langer, Ellen. *Mindfulness*. Reading, MA: Addison-Wesley, 1989.

Norman, Donald. *The Design of Everyday Things*. New York, NY: Doubleday, 1988.

Rubinstein, Moshe F. "From Chaos to Order; Thriving on Change." In *Selected Management Topics*, Vol. 2, Arnold R. Mahachek, ed. Arlington, VA: Association for the Advancement of Medical Instrumentation, 1995.

Rubinstein, Moshe F. *Patterns of Problem Solving*. Englewood Cliffs, NJ: Prentice-Hall, 1975.

Rubinstein, Moshe F. *Tools for Thinking and Problem Solving*. Englewood Cliffs, NJ: Prentice-Hall, 1986.

Rubinstein, Moshe F., and Iris R. Firstenberg. *Patterns of Problem Solving*. Englewood Cliffs, NJ: Prentice-Hall, 1995.

Rubinstein, Moshe F., and Kenneth Pfeiffer. *Concepts in Problem Solving*. Englewood Cliffs, NJ: Prentice-Hall, 1980.

Senge, Peter M. *The Fifth Discipline: The Art and Practice of the Learning Organization*. New York, NY: Doubleday, 1990.

von Hippel, Eric. *The Sources of Innovation*. New York, NY: Oxford University Press, 1988.

Womack, James P., Daniel T. Jones, and Daniel Roos. *The Machine that Changed the World*. New York, NY: Harper Perennial, 1991.

INDEX

ABOUT THE AUTHORS

Moshe F. Rubinstein, Ph.D.

Professor Moshe F. Rubinstein is a professor at the UCLA School of Engineering and Applied Sciences and is Director of the A-B-C Corporate Network at the Anderson Graduate School of Management at UCLA. He is an internationally renowned authority on problem solving and creativity in organizations. He is widely respected for his insights, expertise, and ability to infuse organizations with tools for decision making and innovation. He has been a consultant to many major corporations and has been invited to lecture all over the world.

Professor Rubinstein is a Fulbright Hays fellow and has received numerous awards for his outstanding teaching, including the UCLA Academic Senate Award, the UCLA Alumni Award, and the Anderson School Executive Education Teaching Award. He has written eight books, including *Patterns of Problem Solving*, *Tools for Thinking and Problem Solving*, and

Concepts in Problem Solving, and over 100 articles. His books have been translated into several foreign languages.

Iris R. Firstenberg, Ph.D.

Dr. Firstenberg is an adjunct professor in the UCLA Department of Psychology and is Associate Director of the A-B-C Corporate Network at the Anderson Graduate School of Management at UCLA. She teaches courses on problem solving and decision making in the UCLA Department of Psychology, the School of Engineering and Applied Science, and in Anderson School Executive Programs. Dr. Firstenberg is the recipient of a UCLA Outstanding Teaching Award. She has collaborated with Professor Rubinstein for the last 10 years, teaching seminars for executives and coauthoring two books with him.